Remembering the Riots

a literary anthology

a DSTL Arts publication

Remembering the Riots
a literary anthology

The work in this book was written by students from DSTL Arts' Remembering the Riots creative writing workshop series and the workshop's teaching artists, Jennifer C. Fuentes, Abraham Jaramillo, and Luis Antonio Pichardo. This book was first printed in April, 2017 by DSTL Arts publishing.

Cover Design: Luis Antonio Pichardo

Book Design: Luis Antonio Pichardo

ISBN: 978-1-946081-04-9

10 9 8 7 6 5 4 3 2 1

www.DSTLArts.org

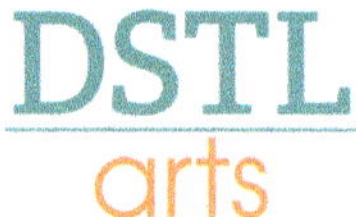

3529 Fletcher Dr.
Los Angeles, CA 90065

To my good sir, for getting me back to my writing.
–Jennifer C. Fuentes

I dedicate this book to all the awfully wonderful people of L.A.; I have learned from them the bad, and certainly the good. Peace and love.
–Abraham Jaramillo

For the community that adopted me, and the community I call home.
–Luis Antonio Pichardo

Table of Contents

From the Balcony

Jennifer C. Fuentes

Inspired to write about the 1992 Los Angeles riots, I became one of three teaching artists teaching a writing workshop entitled "Remembering the Riots" at the Exposition Park Library in South Los Angeles. Although I witnessed the riots from the balcony of my Pico Union apartment as a twelve-year-old, I knew that in order to write a more meaningful and purposeful body of work about the subject, it would be necessary and pivotal to engage another community who also experienced the riots away from a balcony. Every other Saturday, participants walked in excited to share their stories, their fears, their perspectives about a shared history, and every other Saturday I left with the same conclusion: the perspective of the riots I once believed to be accurate and correct was actually limiting.

Our participants taught me that the riots were not only about angry people resisting systematic oppression, but it was also about people that, through looting, were able to get the bag of diapers or two they couldn't afford. Our South Los Angeles participants reminded me of the unity that grew between those that normally wouldn't speak to each other, although neighbors, and that it happens so many times during times of strife. Our South Los Angeles participant's voices are the new voices that have found their way in my work.

Although I lived in a quadruplex apartment in the heart of Pico Union, Los Angeles, I also grew up in South Los Angeles where my parents owned a small Mexican–Salvadorian American restaurant. It was there, on Manchester Boulevard, where I spent my evenings and weekends, riding in my dad's 1983 Toyota Camry on our way to deliver food. I met people who tipped my dad well and people who admitted that they didn't have enough money for a tip. I met a lady who, in broken English, told me how much she admired my middle school penmanship as I was writing an essay while eating a bean and cheese burrito, "I wish I could write that way." I met a man who took out some change and lint from his pocket and asked my mom what he could buy with what he had. I met people who blessed us and prayed for us, and people who told us our food was bland. I met stoic health inspectors that made little eye contact with us, and that we hoped wouldn't see the cockroach crawling on the wall. There were times my mom gave a customer an extra order of fries simply because she knew it was the right thing to do, and there were other times where she was mad at herself for

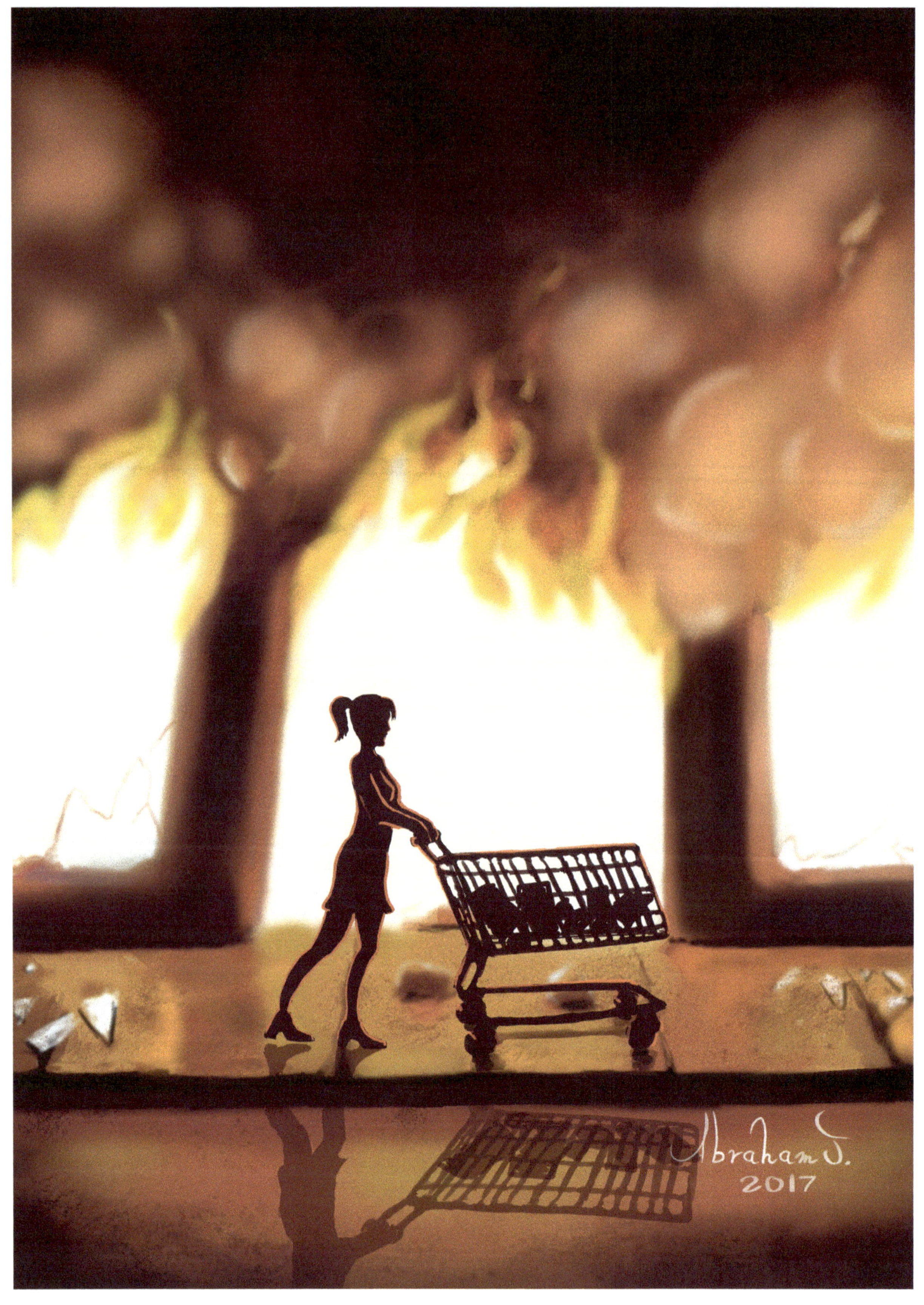

Shopping; *digital illustration*, Abraham Jaramillo

not speaking English well enough to explain to an African American customer that we do, in fact, deliver. She would beat herself up for losing yet another customer until she would see that customer again. In short, every day was different, everyday was full of dynamic, complex people who were doing nothing more than living their life the best way they knew how. Most of them had stories of tired days, of days they wish would pass and hoped would get better. We were in a community with people who did not only walk in for a meal, but people who needed to be heard, who surprised us with gifts, and even those who stole from us. They made us laugh, they even made us cry, sometimes. They were survivors.

And the more we served this South Los Angeles community, the more we learned how much we had in common. Like us, their stories were also important, and like us, their stories were not portrayed accurately. We learned why, for example, one of our customer's teen son had to drop out of school. He had to work after his father got deported to Chihuahua, Mexico. He became more than just a drop out, he became the man of his house. And we learned that our neighbors, owners of a tire shop, had been in business for generations, and even when times were tough, they were resilient enough to keep moving forward. It was also these owners who, when the Los Angeles Riots erupted, taped a "Black Owned" sign to our restaurant window, which saved our little business in the end. In short, South Los Angeles became the community we empathized with because we were them.

It took years at my parents' restaurant to truly learn about a community and understand that what most people lacked in South Los Angeles, like many other communities, was the lack of opportunities to do more than just survive. Most of our customers couldn't thrive because they lacked basic resources, and although they worked harder than anyone, they ended up in the same dead-end cycle: long hours, low wages, high cost of living, little access to education, and the not-so-subtle institutionalized racism that plagued their lives almost daily.

I hope I was able to bring these realities to the page and begin to break some of the misconceptions that affect communities like South Los Angeles. I hope I captured the different voices from South Los Angeles through my short stories, and I hope I helped to create a safe environment where participants were able to express themselves, and write openly and freely. I hope I created an environment where we all listened to our stories and became advocates for ourselves and our neighbors. I hope our residency became a place of empathy and love. I only hope to give readers a glimpse of some of the best years of my life. My years at El Diamante restaurant.

Check Cashing and Liquor Stores

Luis Antonio Pichardo

I didn't grow up in Los Angeles. I'm from the city of Vista, a small suburb of San Diego next to the Marine Corps base, Camp Pendleton. When the riots broke out in L.A. back in April of 1992, I remember watching the images of the Reginald Denny beating on TV over and over again; and I remember seeing images of Black and Brown people looting, burning, and even shooting at first responders. It wasn't a pretty sight. While the National Guard was being mobilized, along with the marines from Camp Pendleton and Miramar Air Force Base, I remember seeing the increase of San Diego County Sheriff's patrol units in my neighborhood. It's like they knew we would be capable of uprising against them too.

You see, living in San Diego, at the time, (and even now, to a certain degree) you were either White, or you were Mexican. It was rare to be something else. And while the reality is that immigrant communities are statistically less likely to engage in criminal activity, there was still plenty for us to be upset about. Surrounded by liquor stores and check cashing spots, we didn't have access to many supermarkets or banks. Redlining of real estate properties and racially-biased lending programs created a barrio that was almost exclusively Mexican, and just like South Central Los Angeles, working class families had to either share an apartment within a beehive of apartment complexes, or get by in a single family home that often housed at least two families. That's exactly how I grew up. And none of that really mattered to me. It was all I knew. But watching that video tape of Rodney King, a Black man, being demolished, nearly beaten to death, by four, White police officers, well, that was scary.

If I had to walk to school everyday, afraid of getting jumped by cholos, I also, now, had to worry about possibly getting beat up by police too. As a child, and a big one for my age, I was already followed by the Korean store owners in my neighborhood. I was already told by White people how articulate I was for someone "like me," which I knew well, even at the age of 9, meant that I was a special kind of Mexican. I was always made to understand my place in the world, but I somehow didn't realize the injustice of it until I saw that tape.

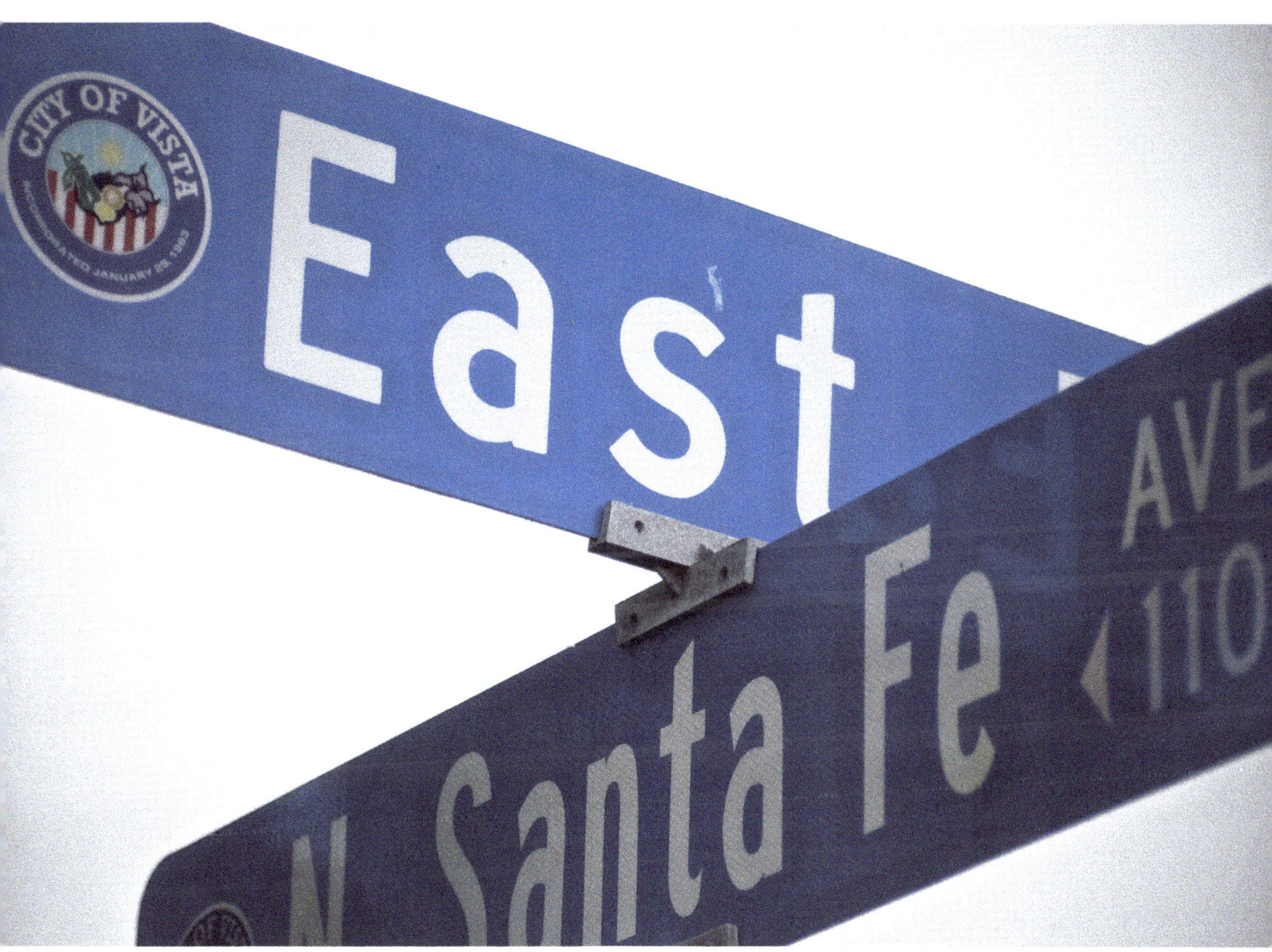

Home; *photograph*, Luis Antonio Pichardo

The year my uncle was murdered at the hands of an ex-lover and her boyfriend in México, and the state police in Querétaro didn't have the "resources" to solve the case, I knew then that I couldn't believe in the police, regardless of where they were from. Watching the L.A. Riots unfold over the course of a week on TV left me with a clear understanding of the value my community had in the eyes of law enforcement and politicians. It was also reinforced by the school system, the shop owners in my neighborhood, and pretty much all White people I had to interact with when translating things for my dad. My mom, being a first-generation "Chicana" knew this well too, and she always made sure to soften the blow for me, but this event gave it to me raw.

I am not like most people. This is true. As an artist, I consider myself, and my role in the art world, as one of a leader. It's my responsibility to create change through the arts, and to empower others to do the same. That's why I founded DSTL Arts, the organization that hosted, in partnership with the Exposition Park Regional Branch Library, the "Remembering the Riots" creative writing workshop series. That is why I believe in teaching others to find their voice through the creative process, and ultimately creating a platform for themselves to share their stories. As the leader of DSTL Arts, I also believe in opening doorways that are often closed to underrepresented communities and artists, and that is why we are publishing this book.

Collected here are not just the stories and artwork of the teaching artists involved in providing this platform to our local, Los Angeles community members. Collected in this book is the voice of the community that lived through the 1992 L.A. Riots, both inside and outside of the place and time period. We are continuing to live the L.A. Riots in some form or another, whether politically, socially, or economically. While the L.A. neighborhoods that were partially razed have changed in appearance, and even been updated, many of the issues that created the environment and catalyst of L.A. Riots have remained the same. Social and racial injustices continue to happen. We can't deny that. And as long as the needs of working class people don't get met with a genuine empathy and policies that truly benefit the poor, we will eventually see another uprising again. It began in Watts in the '60s, occurred again in the '90s, and has potential to happen again in the '10s should our administrations neglect our people, all of our people.

The fact of the matter is, we don't want things to continue to be the same.

Yes, Let's Do This

Abraham Jaramillo

I am a multimedia artist who volunteers for the DSTL Arts program "Conchas y Café," a writing workshop, and when Luis, the executive director of DSTL Arts, asked me if I wanted to take part in this new program called "Remembering The Riots" I got really excited and said, "yes, let's do this!"

I love history and the 1992 L.A. Riots is a really important event in U.S. history that, on the surface, appears like random acts of violence, but once you look deeper into the whole story, it clearly becomes the result of more complex and deep issues.

I didn't experience this event in history, and I began this project with the intent of learning and acquiring insight from the participants of these workshops whom lived through and experienced the riots.

With this new perspective, I proceeded to write, draw, photograph, and take action.

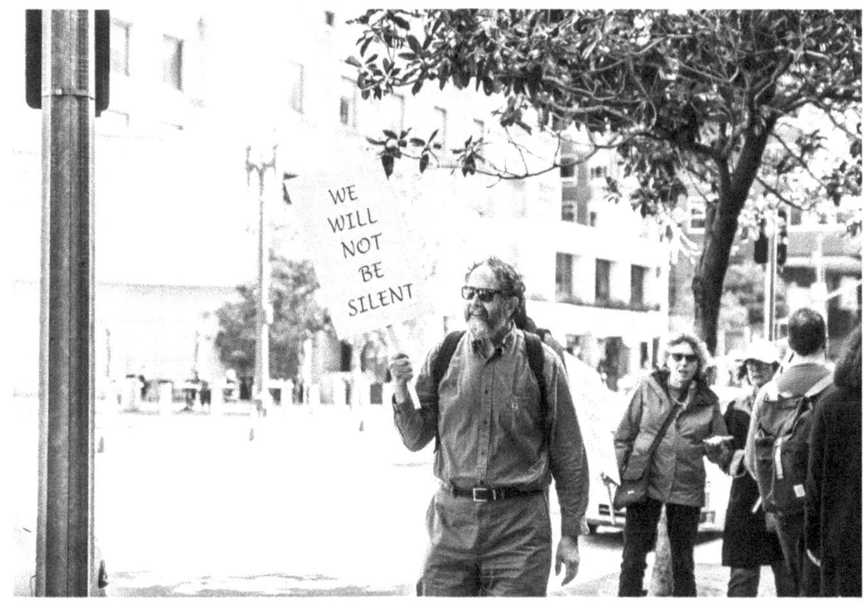

"The forces that create a riot also manifest themselves in the form of 'visual protest.'"; *photograph*, Abraham Jaramillo

1992 L.A. Riots

(a key)

A. March 3, 1991, Rodney King was severely beaten and arrested by five Los Angeles Police Department officers: Stacey Koon, Laurence Powell, Timothy Wind, Theodore Briseno, and Rolando Solano.

B. April 29, 1992, all four officers charged with crimes related to police brutality were acquitted; a protest formed outside of the L.A. County Courthouse in Downtown L.A.

C. Looting and acts of violence, including the beating of two truck drivers, Larry Tarvin, and famously, Reginald Denny, erupt at the intersection of Florence and Normandie.

D. At the Parker Center Heliport, L.A.P.D. Headquarters in Downtown L.A., protesters turned violent and initiated further rioting action, blocking the 101 FWY.

E. Day 2; rioting spread to Koreatown, a curfew was enacted by Mayor Tom Bradley, and the National Guard was deployed. One of our teaching artists lived through the riots in Pico Union.

F. One of our workshop participants was in Santa Barbara, on a school-related field trip, when rioting began.

G. One of our workshop participants was living in San Diego when rioting began.

H. One of our workshop participants lived in Pomona, witnessing riots, there, firsthand.

I. One of our workshop participants was in Torrance when rioting began.

J. One of our workshop participants was on 29th and Crenshaw, witnessing the riots firsthand

Z. Marines were deployed from Camp Pendleton to quell the riots. One of our teaching artists lived in the neighboring city.

map by: Abraham Jaramillo

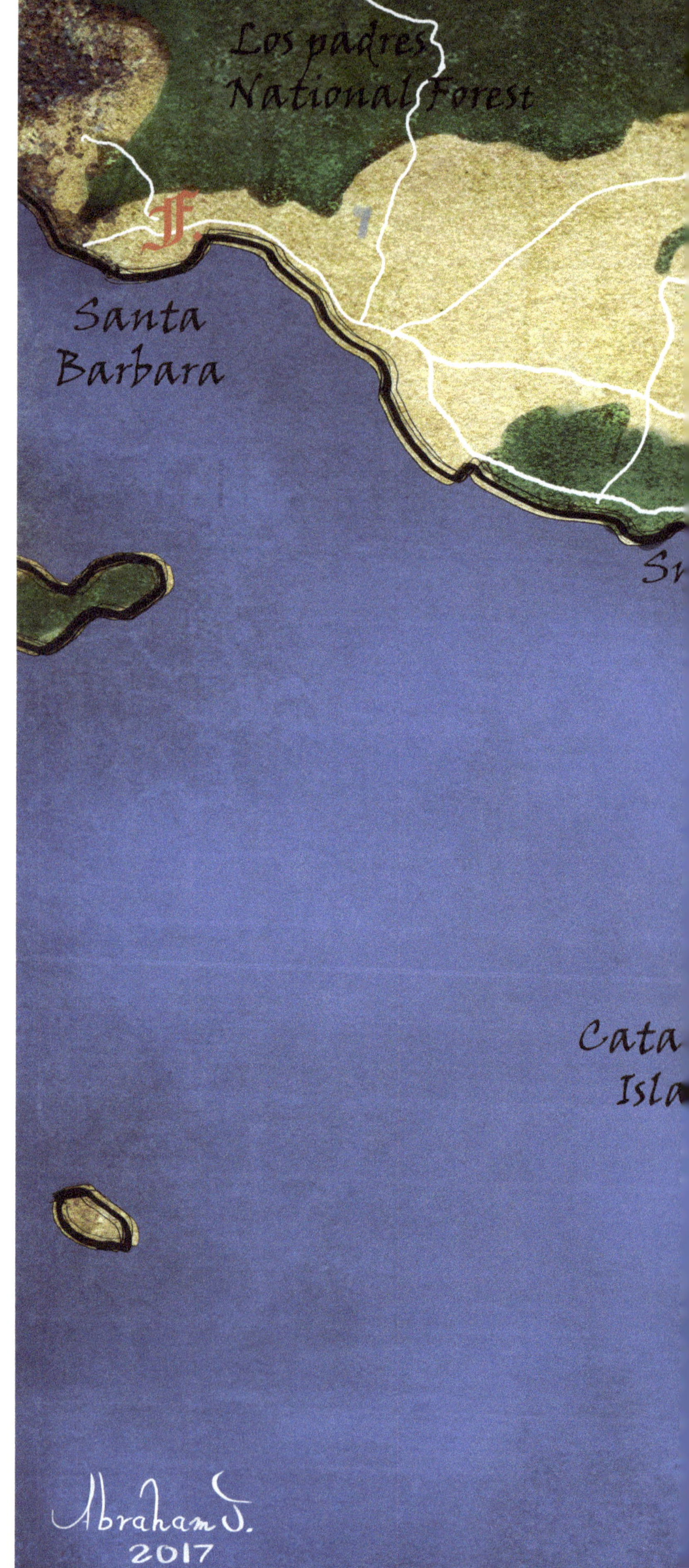

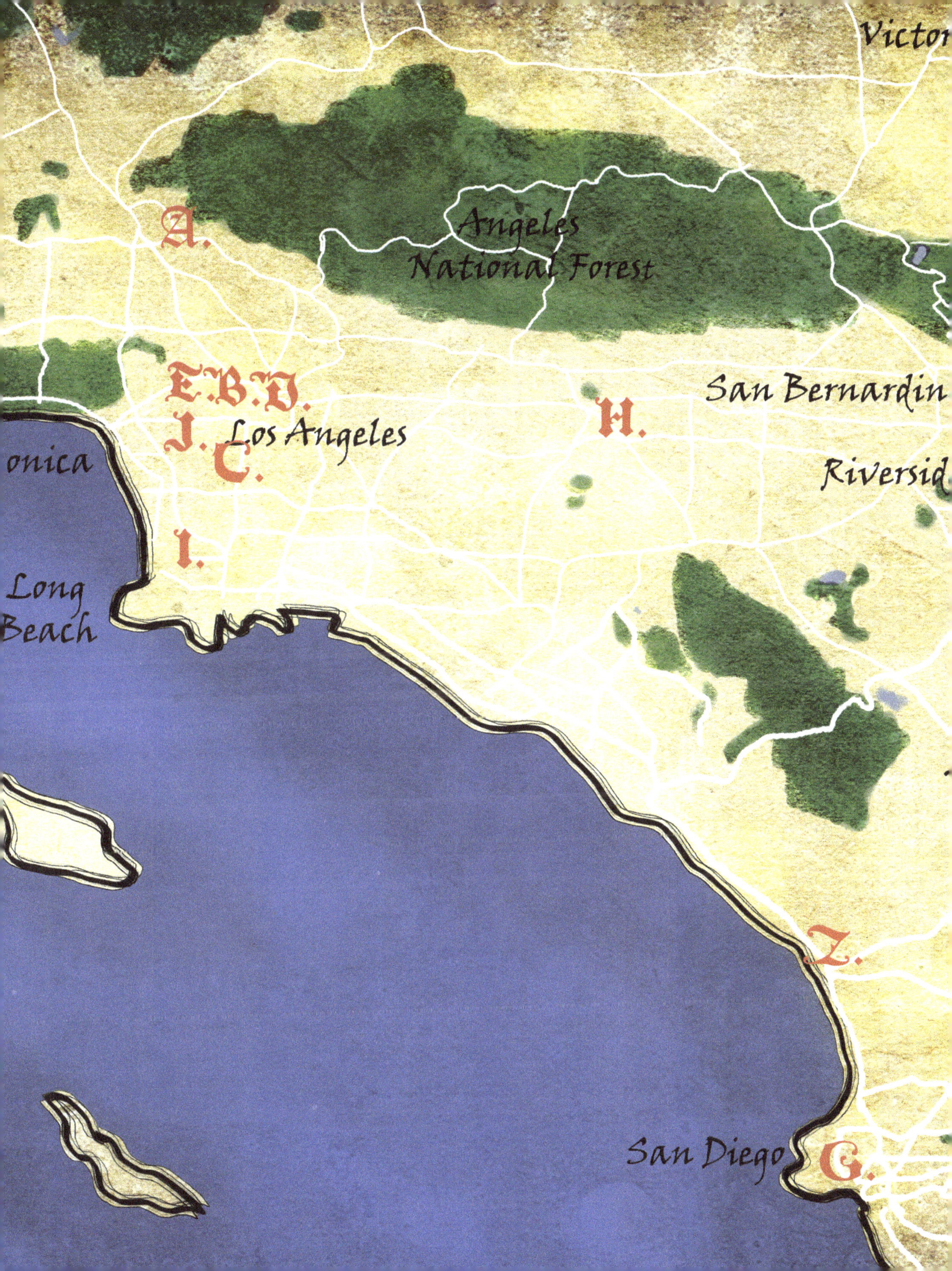
Victor
Angeles
National Forest
A.
E.B.D.
J.
C.
Los Angeles
H.
San Bernardin
Riversid
onica
I.
Long
Beach
Z.
San Diego
G.

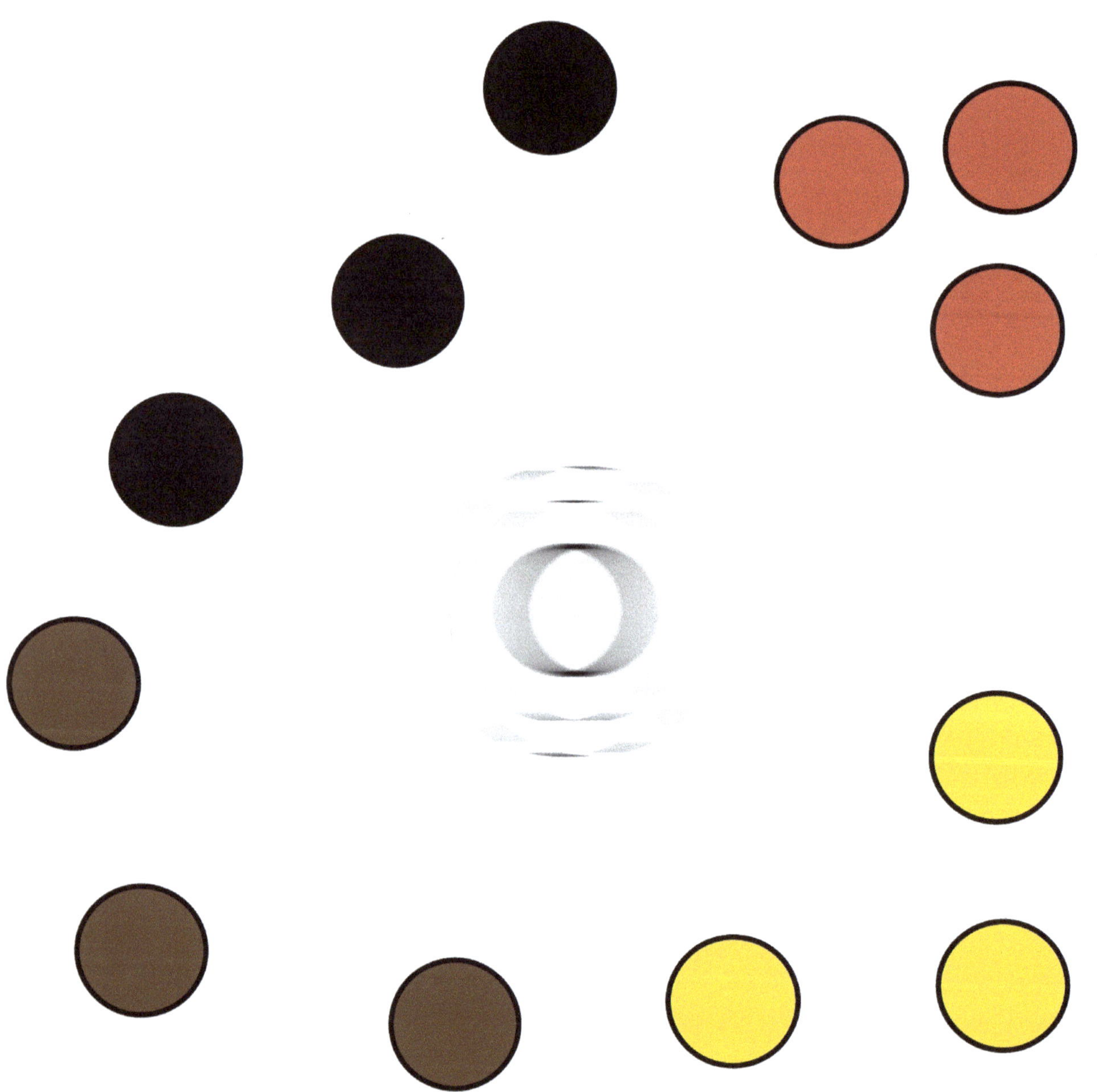

Dots; *digital illustration*, Abraham Jaramillo

Mr. Trimis

Jennifer C. Fuentes

Mr. Trimis was my 7th grade music teacher in 1992. He was a tall, white, and sloppy man who ate a Snickers bar and a Coke for breakfast in the mornings; he wore brown polyester pants on a daily basis, and never tied his shoe laces. He must have been very poor, because he only had two pairs of shoes: a pair of dirty and worn out Asics, and a pair of leather boat shoes riddled with holes.

"Sir, your toe is sticking out."

"Mind your business, young lady."

Trimis acted like he was mad at us, but we all knew he more than tolerated us annoying middle schoolers. He was, for example, the only teacher that allowed kids to hang out with him in the mornings, during nutrition, and lunch. He didn't care for his "adult" time, which most teachers considered sacred. He, instead, used all the time he could to teach us everything about our instruments. It was in the mornings that he taught me the art of vibrato and third position on my violin. There he was, shoulder-length, dirty-blonde hair covering part of his face, modeling the graceful movement of fingers on strings in between bites of his Snickers and short Coke sips. He'd model a few times and then have me practice.

"Remember, Concert Master, you got to learn this stuff in order to teach the rest."

"Aren't you the teacher?"

"Aren't you the Concert Master, or would you rather give up your seat?"

"Alright, Jesus, I get it."

"Go to class, and you're not funny!" he'd say as he put his hair in a pony tail.

Rumor had it that Trimis could play every single musical instrument ever invented—even the recorder. This I believed, because although he was not one to brag, I remember hearing his melodic and soothing notes make their way into my sterile math class a few windows away. While Mr. Chung, my fat and sweaty math teacher yelled at us for not understanding algebraic expressions, Trimis' notes filled my soul like the comfort of eating a crumbled Twix bar in french vanilla ice cream. Sometimes I took in the glory of the piano, soldiers coming home safe and sound from a long and difficult battle. Other times, I was taken by the seductive saxophone and the man suffering terribly from an unrequited love. And still, other times, the agony of the cello or viola reminded me of my dad's defeated face on my way to the operating room to get rid me of my appendix when I was in the 3rd grade. Trimis was unaware that most days he not only made me forget my oppressive math class, but he also transported me out of my insignificant middle school experience. He was more than a middle school teacher: he was a storyteller that taught me to reflect on, and escape from, at least for a little bit, all that was confusing in the 7th grade.

"Fuentes, are you paying attention?"

"Yes, sir."

It was of no surprise, the day after the L.A. riots broke out and our school was in disarray, that Trimis had us, nonetheless, practicing.

"But sir, my mom is about to pick me up," said a lazy, 8th grade cellist who should have been taking wood shop instead.

"She's not here now, is she?

"What about the fire, sir?" I asked.

"The school is not on fire, is it?"

"Why don't we put the news on. That's what Mr. Chung did last period," said another.

"We will play until the principal comes to evacuate us, not before! Now, get your instruments out and stop the complaining! We will continue to move forward."

His face was flushed; the green and purple veins on his temples protruded, never had I seen so much color on his pale face before. He tied his hair in a pony tail and tied his air conditioned boat shoes. The latter, a first.

"Please tune your own instruments today," he said. We said not a word.

We followed suit and tuned our string orchestra. Although he did this for us everyday while sitting at his piano, and almost always scolded us for the excess rosin on our finger boards, we knew today was the day to keep our mouths shut. He didn't smile, he didn't call us ladies and germs like he always did. He stood behind his podium, quietly waiting for us despite the fact that some of us struggled with pushing our pegs in and keeping them in place, or that some still couldn't hear a correctly pitched A. The screeching, winding and plucking of strings did not affect Trimis, neither did the hollering outside our door, nor the fast-running L.A Gears and teacher heels. The tuning slowly began to subside, but the chaos outside grew louder. Was this how I was going to die, in my school's music room with my very poor and stubborn, music teacher? With this Jesus look-alike?

I remembered the man that was taken out of his truck and almost beaten to death the night before. Did he die? Shouldn't we be talking about that instead? Shouldn't we be talking about the fires and the thieves, and the Korean I saw early in the morning on my way to school with his shot gun on the roof top of his furniture store? What about El Diamante? The restaurant my parents had worked so hard for? Would it even be around when all this was over? And where was my mom? She should have picked me up already. Could something have happened to her? Music couldn't be more important than talking about our city at war. There were knocks and banging on the classroom door, but no one dared to open it. We were all perfectly paralyzed, seated with our perfect performance postures, sheet music ready, violins on our laps. The smell of smoke invaded our senses; squealing sirens in close proximity and the now constant and persistent banging of the door. We heard keys, and someone opened the door, but I didn't dare turn around to see who it was. A silent, "Oh, sorry." And the door closed again. I was definitely held hostage. And Trimis stood silently, baton in hand, gaze at his shoes. What was wrong with this man?

He looked up, baton in his right hand. We got into playing position. No one dared ask what we were going to play. Students shifted and looked through their sheet music but he shook his head. I had "My Favorite Things" on the stand and assumed this was Trimis' chosen piece, since this is what we had been practicing lately. I was Concert Master, and it was my duty to guide, especially now that this man had lost his mind. I mouthed it to the cello section and the second violins, and assumed those first violinists behind me could see the music on my stand. Right before Trimis moved his baton, he winked at me and said to us all, "Play your hearts out, and do it well."

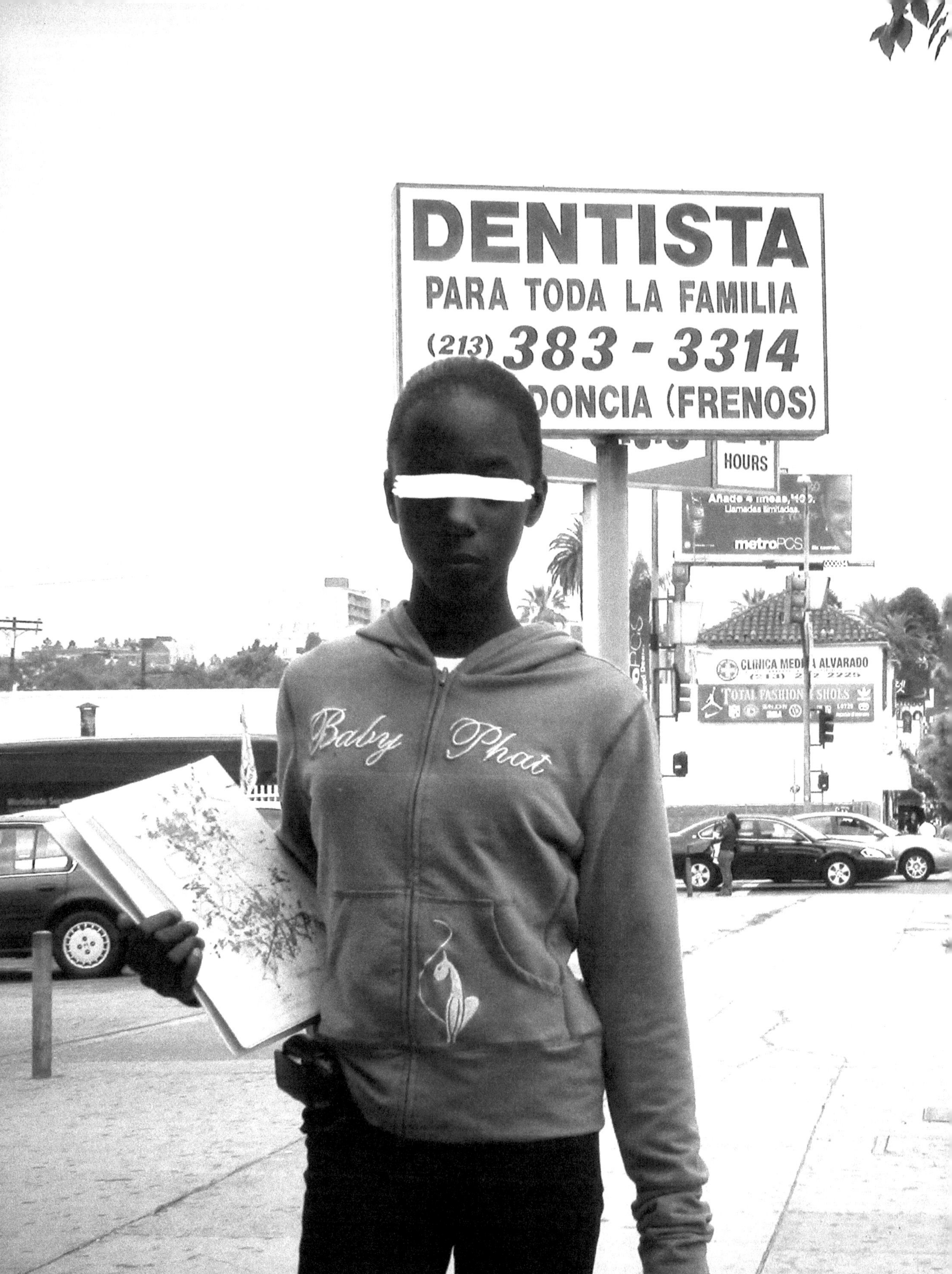
DENTISTA
PARA TODA LA FAMILIA
(213) 383 - 3314
DONCIA (FRENOS)
HOURS
metroPCS
ALVARADO
Baby Phat

Who Cares for The Soul of Soul People?

Mello "Bluez" Houston

Blues music is more than laughs & fun & sexy situations.

Blues is deeper than fat hog on a "slave's" table on a holiday.

Blues music is actually full of neglected people's real tears..

Not the "good times" only music. Not the big laugh "I wanna do something freaky to you" only stuff… No. Real blues has sweat & blood memories. No ish. Yes. People need to stop playing with their forebears freedom music & get real even for 1 day…

Baby Phat (modified); *digital illustration*, Luis Antonio Pichardo

That

Tina Fallon

Webster's defines: *diverse*, modif — Syn. several, assorted, different, distinct. See *different*.

Different, modif. 1. Unlike in nature.

I was interviewing for a substitute teaching position for L.A.U.S.D. (Los Angeles Unified School District). The Talent Acquisition Specialist asked the question, after several businessy questions: "Are you comfortable working with diverse students?" Diverse. THAT word stuck in me like a dart! What was she talking about? I have worked in Special Education for about 10 or 12 years...? Is this to find out if I am a racist? I am, by the way, going to work in Los Angeles. People come from all over the world just to visit! Some actually live there! Wait a minute, is this because I'm WHITE? Can't be. I'm not that white... Is my skin that color that people may refer to as 'caucasian.' I thought I was Italian/Irish? Or does that fall under the category of 'caucasian'? I can't even spell CAUCASIAN, I had to use spell check to find out! But that word 'diverse'? If you looked up DIVERSE in Wikipedia, you wouldn't find an image of me in the description!

Who EXACTLY is she speaking... of?? Does she think that I prefer to live in a land, in a la la land of like-colored skin types? And was she ready IF I had said, 'No, thank you! Like, I want to work at a place where people are more like me and not like, like you. And I'm not, like, saying this because you're black or anything like that... so? What I am saying is that, um... like this job-thing is like, not for me! Sure, it pays well, but I didn't come here to be diverse!" Then I would flip my hair and add; "I have seen lots of Black, Hispanic, Asian, Armenian, and others on TV, I just didn't know that they were in the schools, too?!" And she would think that I was so sad because now I would realize that I could not step out of my home and NOT walk amongst persons of my size, my shape, and especially my color (whatever that may be) and be myself??

Where do I find the people who look like me? Just like me! Caucasian, like me?

But the real question, if I had been Hispanic or black or even Pacific Islander, would I have been asked that question? I feel awkward and uncomfortable! Should I be complaining? Yes, I should! Because we are all DIVERSE. This should not have been a question or an issue! Should it? Diverse is exciting. Am I not also diverse?

And what is the opposite of diverse?

Antonym: Alike,

like,

similar.

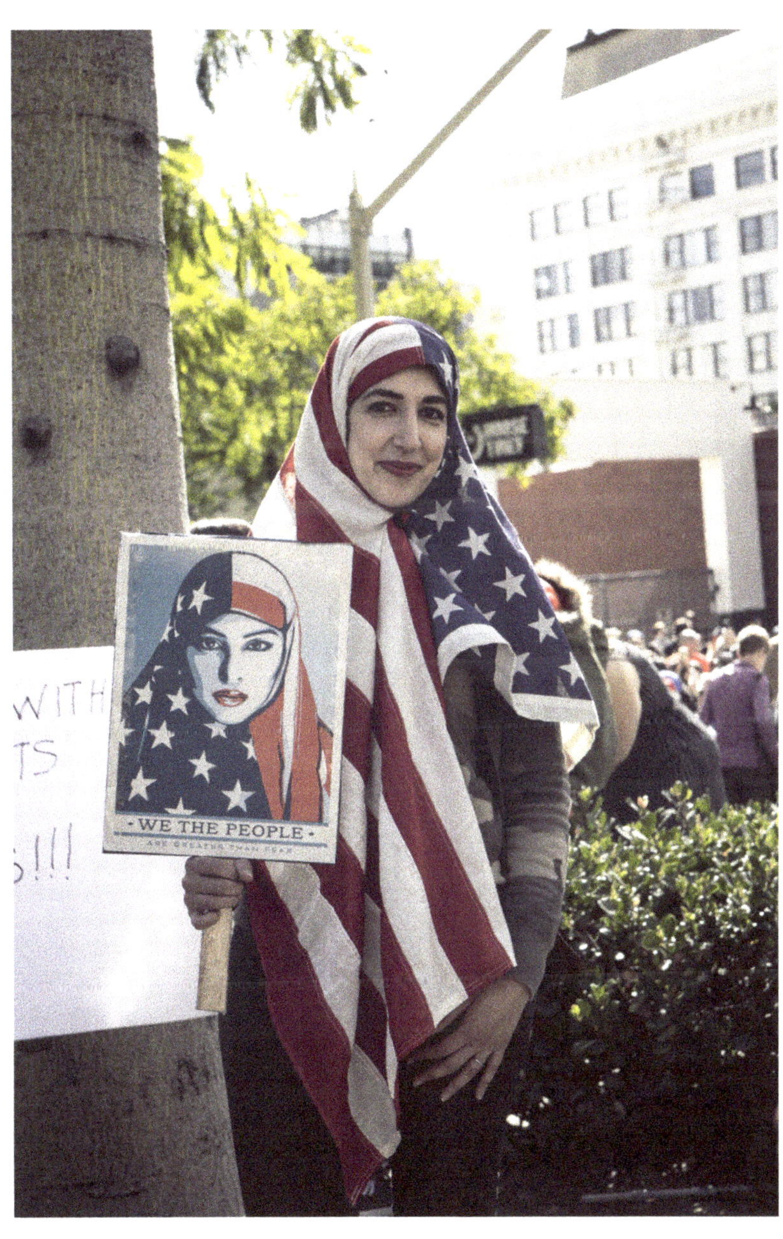

Women's March #1; *photograph*, Abraham Jaramillo

Melanin Infected

Luis Antonio Pichardo

The Korean at the 99 cent
kept following me.
I left my handful
of deodorant sticks and
travel-size mouthwashes,
frustrated.

The Jakartan liquor store
stopped carrying
my favorite mazapán
because no one cared
to keep the last Latino
product, preferring
only Japanese peanuts and
craft IPAs in the mid-Wilshire
hood.

The Vietnamese laundromat
fucked up my jacket,
claiming I should've dry
cleaned that shit,
but the label clearly said
Machine Wash in Cold
Water.

The pregnant white
woman downtown moved
closer to the light
as I left the intersection
clearly scared I might infect

her with my melanin
and ruin her privileged
child.

I'm tired.
Who else doesn't
want to connect with
me?

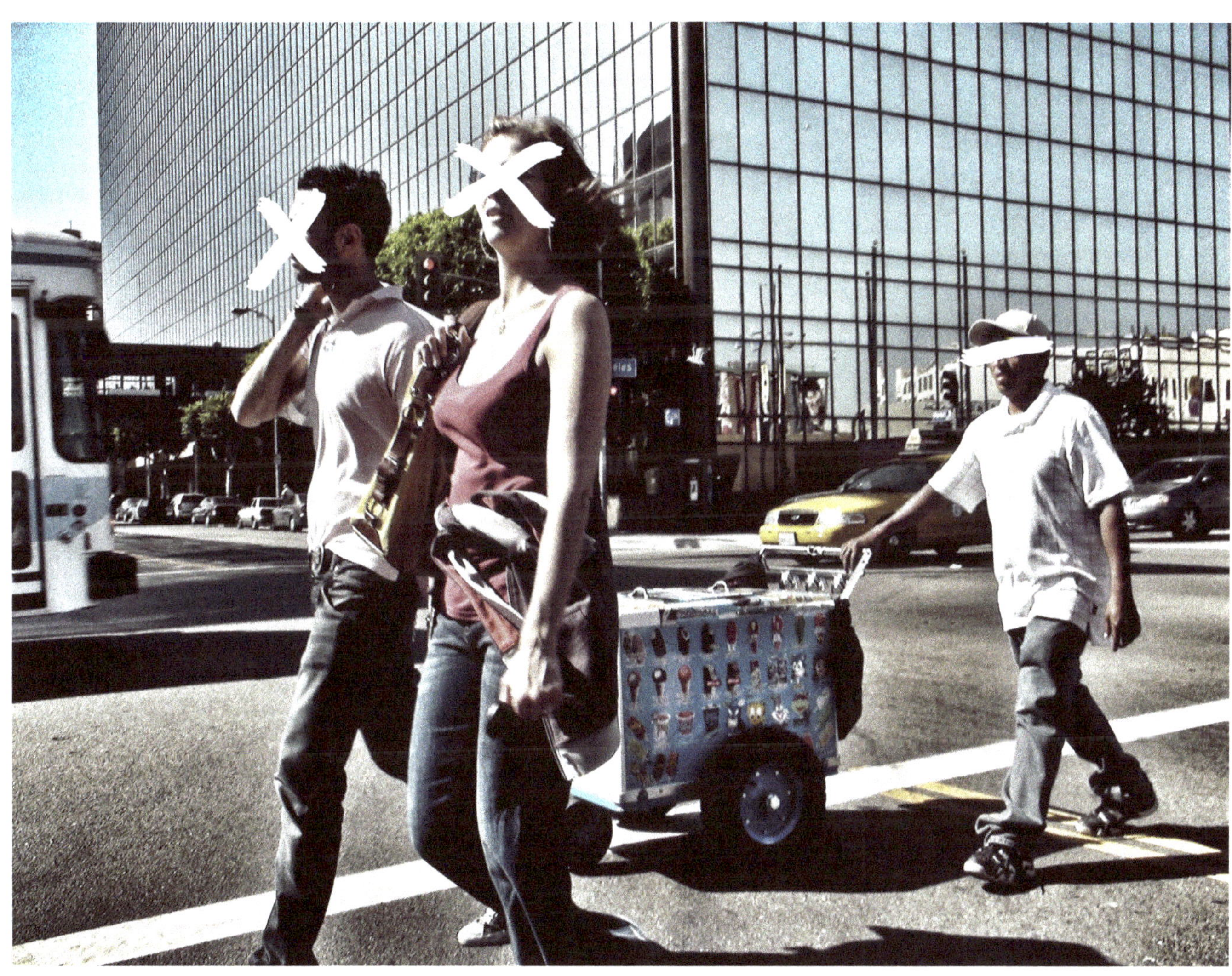

Divides; *digital illustration*, Luis Antonio Pichardo

Day Two of L.A. Riots, 1992

Maggie Kane

Repeating images on TV news.
Full scale riots, day two.
Dusk to dawn, Los Angeles curfew.

National Guard, police, firefighters.
Walkie-talkies, phones, radios, radar;
helicopters trucks, tanks, cars.

Oozing, yellowing overhanging clouds.
No route a quicker way.
No one wants to be on the streets of L.A.

Bumper to bumper traffic.
Hours and hours to get a few miles.
Grim, frozen faces; nobody smiles.

Up in the Santa Monica Mountains,
the view from Mt. St. Mary's College.
I am leaning over the car park ledge.

23 plumes of smoke and fires.
East, South, West L.A., ablaze.
The skies a somber, smoky haze.

Everybody wants an earthquake kit.
No preparation, no guidebook.
Before, inward eyes, now an outward look.

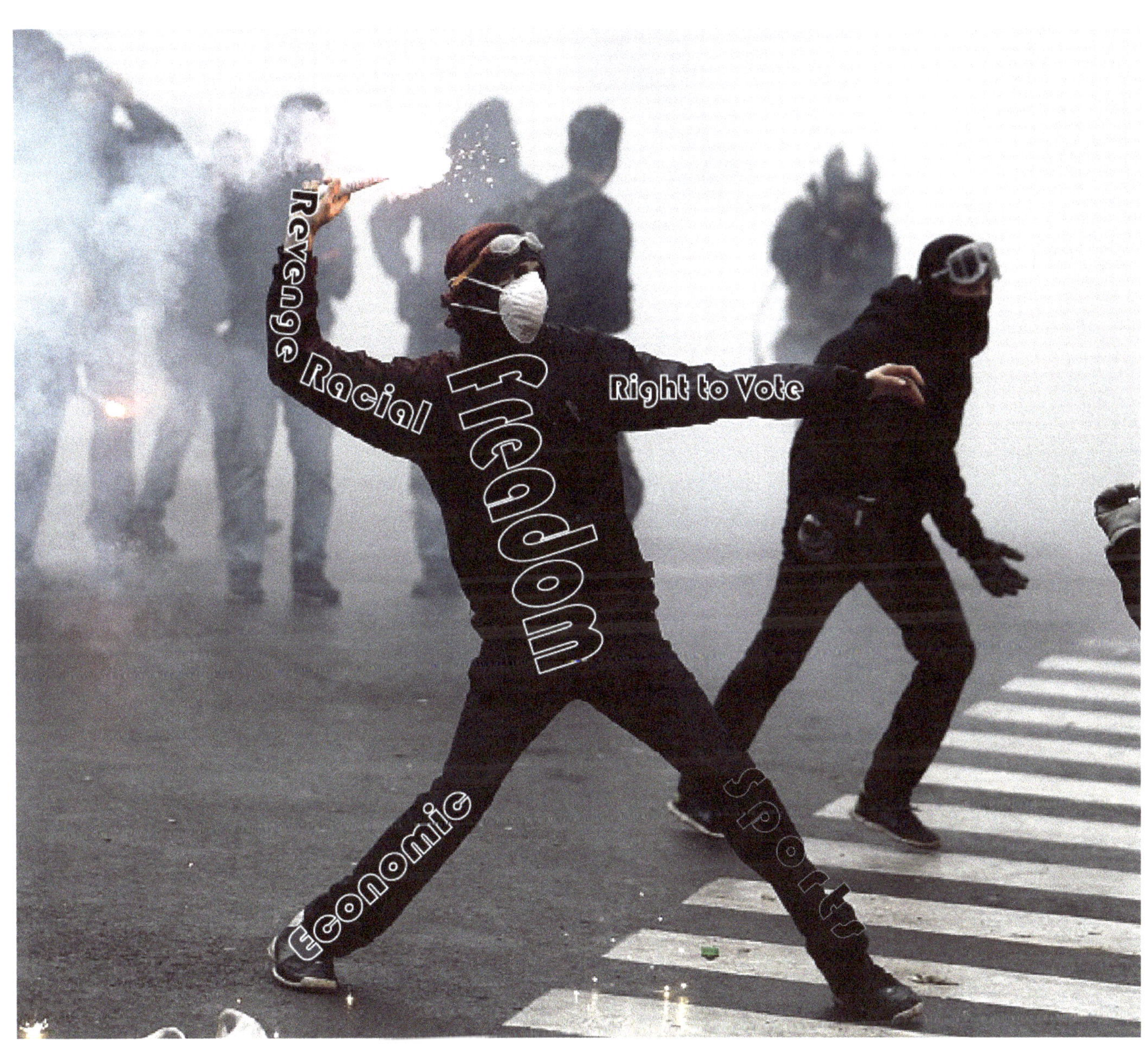

Riot Smoke; *digital illustration*, Abraham Jaramillo

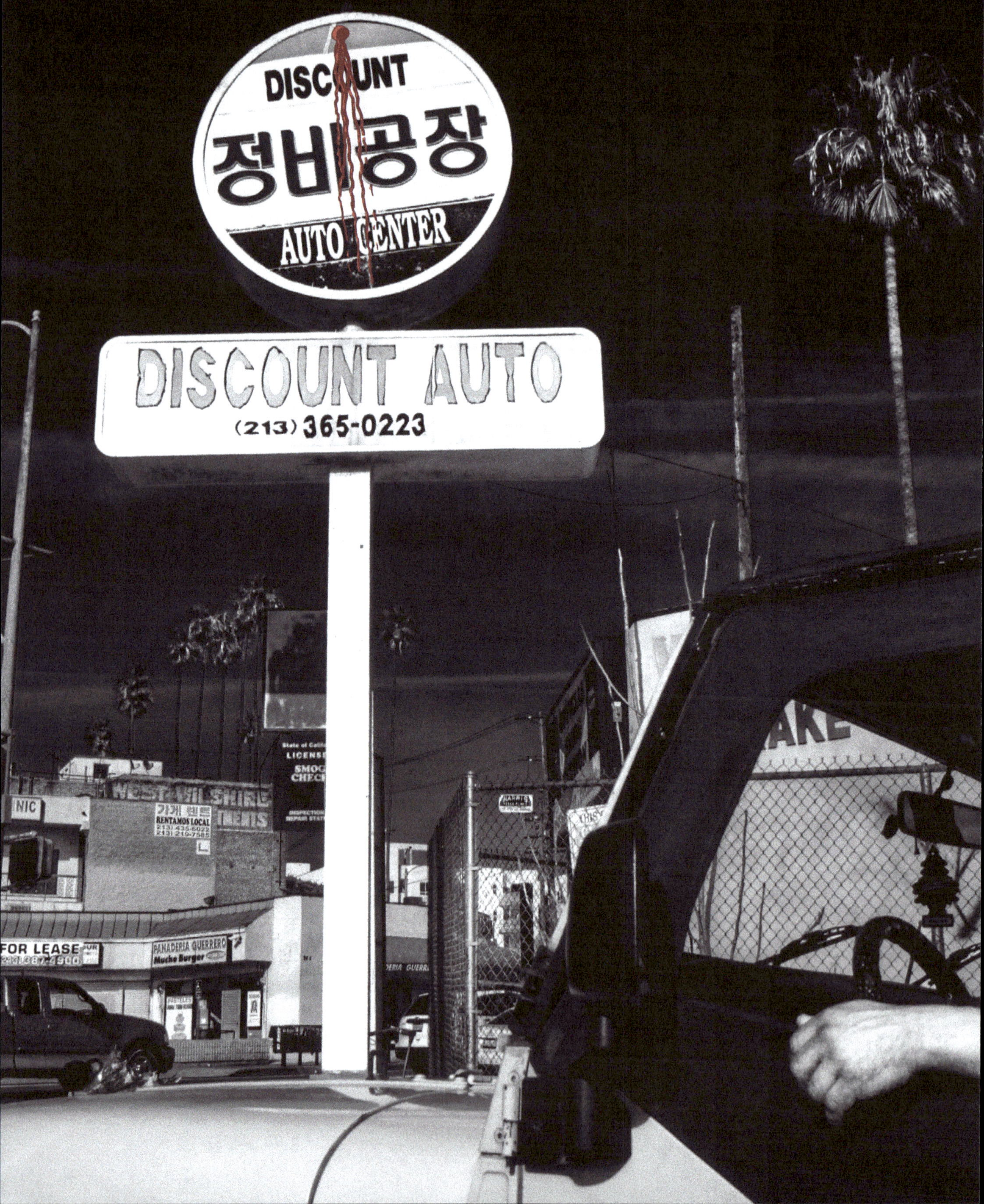

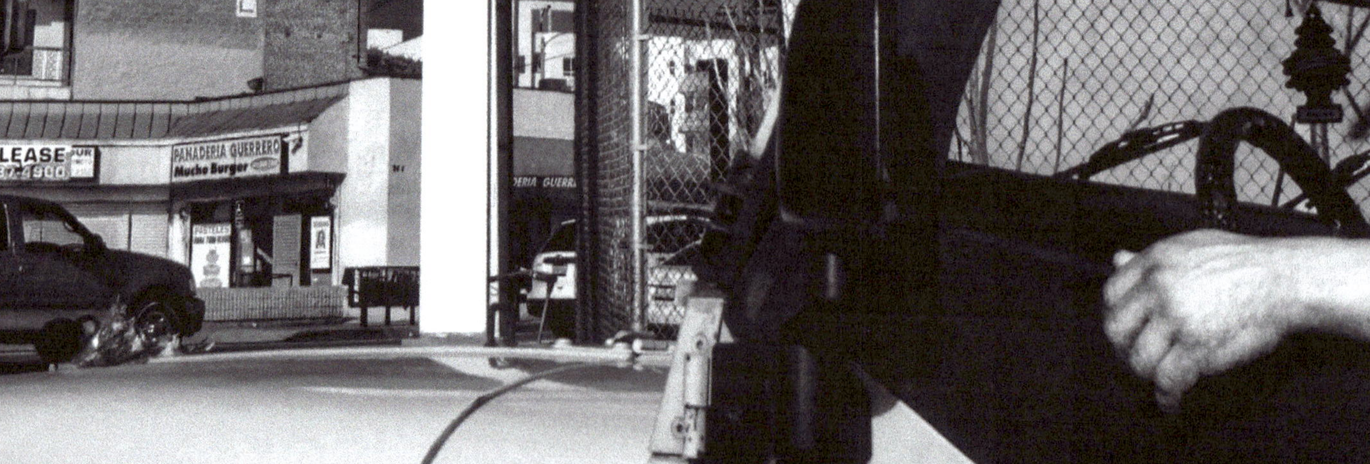
DISCOUNT
정비공장
AUTO CENTER
DISCOUNT AUTO
(213) 365-0223
FOR LEASE
PANADERIA GUERRERO
Mucho Burger

April 29th, 1992

Mello "Bluez" Houston

April 29th, 1992. Walking north on our street then; 3rd Avenue from Rodeo Road

To Jefferson Blvd I could feel the tension in the air over the Rodney King event

& the policemen's total acquittal. Going to The Reggae "Church"

where some socially conscious Musicians & writers would be.

Walking in disbelief of society's confusion & combustible

Inequalities. We drove out of the city to the outskirts. Later, turned on the TV & seen a city burning. Shocked & yet, experiencing surprising unity among the inner-city "everyday people" to quote 1960s rock & roll icon Sly Stone. Thinking about his song "Stand" as well...

Headshot; *digital illustration*, Luis Antonio Pichardo

Watching T.V., Waiting on The Verdict

Luis Antonio Pichardo

I hear the neighbors
through the walls that listen,
argue,
who's bringing diapers
home tonight after
work because Abby
can't use naturals,
nothing natural,
in any sense, but
he says, I can't,
but $4 in cash for
the bus to work,
the bus home,
and she can't with
her $10 for gas
and grocery, cuz baby
gotta eat first.

And it happens.
We all hear.

Not guilty.

All counts.

Not guilty.

Arguments stop.

Silence.

I watch ABC dumb-
founded in boxers:
no work, no clothes-day.
Too many of these
lately.

We all stay silent.

Even video
can be beat.

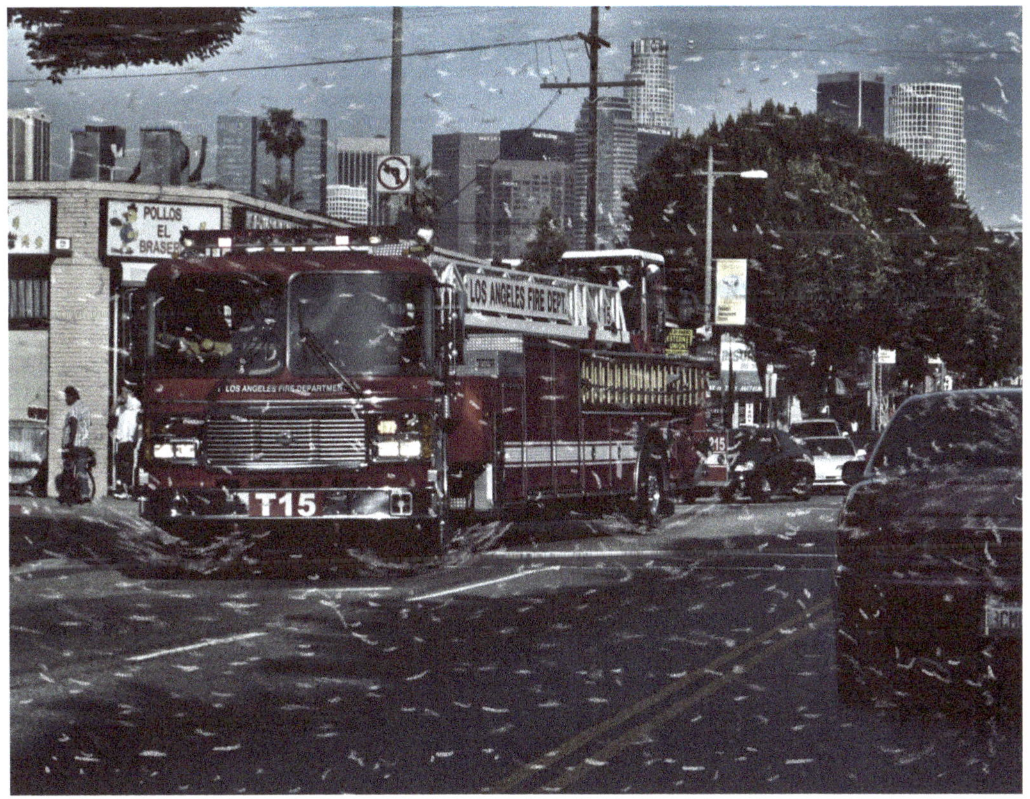

Ashes Reign; *digital illustration*, Luis Antonio Pichardo

Riot

eternal amber
insatiable wildfire
the people ignite

Riot; *digital illustration/haiku*, Abraham Jaramillo

In 1992 Reggae Music Was The Blues We Danced To

Mello "Bluez" Houston

the tropical spirit, up from the islands had the answer of peace

& organic bread; we played by the ocean in L.A.; Venice beach

& poetry helped sooth the beasts in we, shook-up from crying about hard-to-get world peace & nobody wanted to cry. our poems were jagged & lots of expletives & some yelling to ourselves like lost sheeps in lions colors… where's the jungle in the city. Mandella got out & we ran to the Coliseum & DANCED. people checked in school. time for college again, but this time will be the charm. something has to give & these streets still ring out shots & the classy bunch just shot whiskey some will think but there's no relief just yet is it? the tropical truth from the reggae singers of-post-Obama Spring forward Be

"One Love. Be yourself in the best light you can breath."

Go beyond simple be leaf… Be tree…

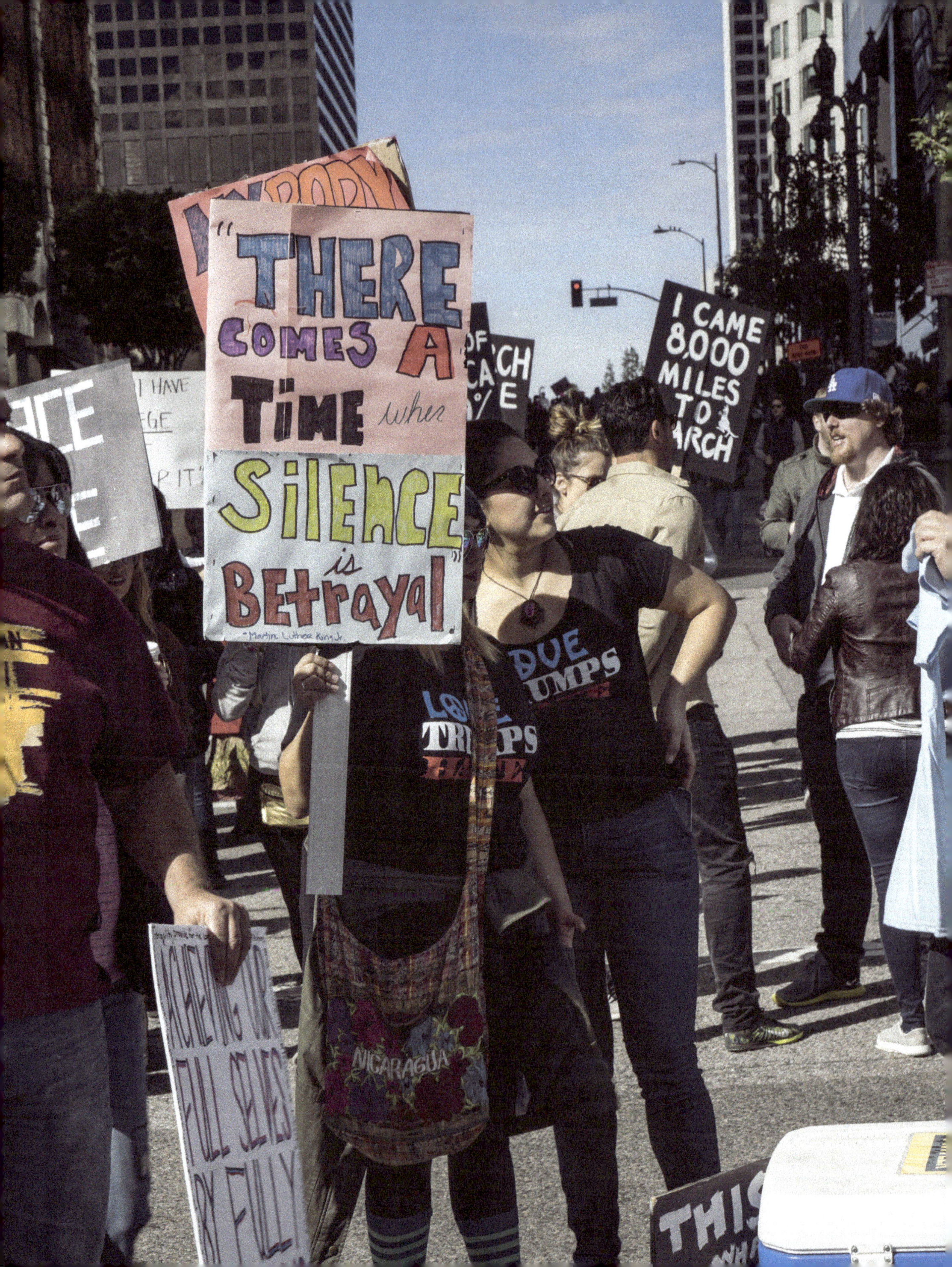
"THERE COMES A TIME when Silence is Betrayal"
Martin Luther King Jr.
I CAME 8,000 MILES TO ARCH
NICARAGUA
THIS

Silence

David Fallon

when they silence you
take away your voice
they take away your choice

when they quiet you
they brew in you
the fear to speak

when they hush you
they push you down
make you weak

when you break the silence
they crack
you take your power back
transform chains
into winds of change
express who you
are meant to be

when you break the silence
you set yourself free

Women's March #7; *photograph*, Abraham Jaramillo

Brick

Abraham Jaramillo

Interesting it is
rigid, quiet,
unanimated object it is
cold, does not feel or think
just an object, is it?
(((BOOM)))
The silence is broken
heavy, ridged and sharp
it chipped and blood ran out
still cold, does not feel or think
just an object, is it?

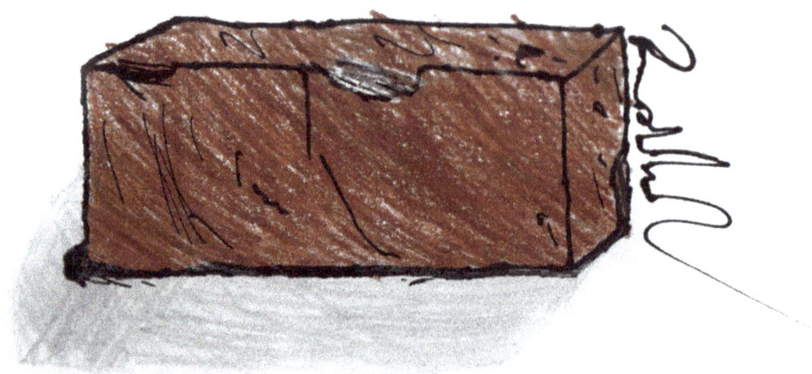

Brick; *ink and colored pencil illustration*, James Fallon

Profanity

Michelle Smith

Can you cuss like a sailor?
Are your words sharp as a razor?
Do they sting like a bee or a gun of a tazer?
Profanity,
A word sandwich thickly layered
Poppin' like Flaming Cheetos in your mouth.
Full of flavor,
Maybe unwavered,
And a habit unsavored.
Profanity,
Profanity,
Excessive or Expressive,
but full of labor.

A Brown Couch

Jennifer C. Fuentes

My dad was determined to get us out of our old quadruplex as soon as possible the day the L.A. Riots broke out. Our quadruplex stood on busy Vermont Avenue, a block from Washington Boulevard, next to a furniture store, across the street from a Thrifty's Drug Store, a 20/20 Video store, and a small market.

My parents, sister and I didn't know we were in trouble until we saw our busy street on TV. We ran to our balcony and witnessed tornadoes of people pushing and shoving their way into the Thrifty's, while some casually walked out with boxes of diapers, tubs of ice cream, and what looked like cough syrup. People ran out of the small market with bags of carrots and cigarettes. I stood at the balcony of my apartment in a trance, unable to move. I saw my 7th grade classmates. I saw the neighbors. I saw people I regularly saw on the streets and on the bus; people determined to take enough to feed their families for at least a couple of days. My entire community came together that April 30, 1992.

Mr. Kim, the furniture store owner, attempted to save his business with a shotgun. He stood on his store's roof top and pointed his weapon at the crowd. But no one cared about Mr. Kim because people made their way into his store and took all that they could. People came out with couches, tables and chairs; a long centipede of headless men with heavy furniture on their backs. There was a plethora of anger, opportunity and boredom. And soon enough the furniture store went up in flames. Mr. Kim disappeared. The flames were taunting us, warming our windows.

"Quickly, let's start packing, we're next!" my dad instructed.

And so he wrapped our VHS player in a beach towel and started loading the car. "We have to get out what's most important," he said.

I followed orders and started packing his tapes, his records. I made sure to pocket my stashed lipsticks, just in case. Our apartment's windows were getting hotter. The tips of the flames were gently caressing my childhood home.

And while the cops raided our street and took their batons out, beating anyone in their way, two neighborhood boys climbed the small hill up Vermont with a couch on their back. They would occasionally stop to adjust and then continue on their way.

They climbed up the hill, slowly, taking breaks whenever they could. I, back at my balcony, could see that the climb was becoming steeper: snails now, safe from the crowd. They slowed their pace more and more, a heavy burden. From where they were, I imagined they could see little fires, cockroaches and ants. They were almost up the hill, almost there…

At the top of the hill, at the very top, one of them tripped and his hands slipped. The couch tumbled down the hill, down the middle of the street, hitting cars; down, down.

At the bottom of the hill, rioters wrestled with each other and destroyed the couch in the process. I walked back inside, having forgotten my packing duties, when on TV I saw my dad standing on the roof of our quadruplex, watering our roof with a garden hose, determined to save us.

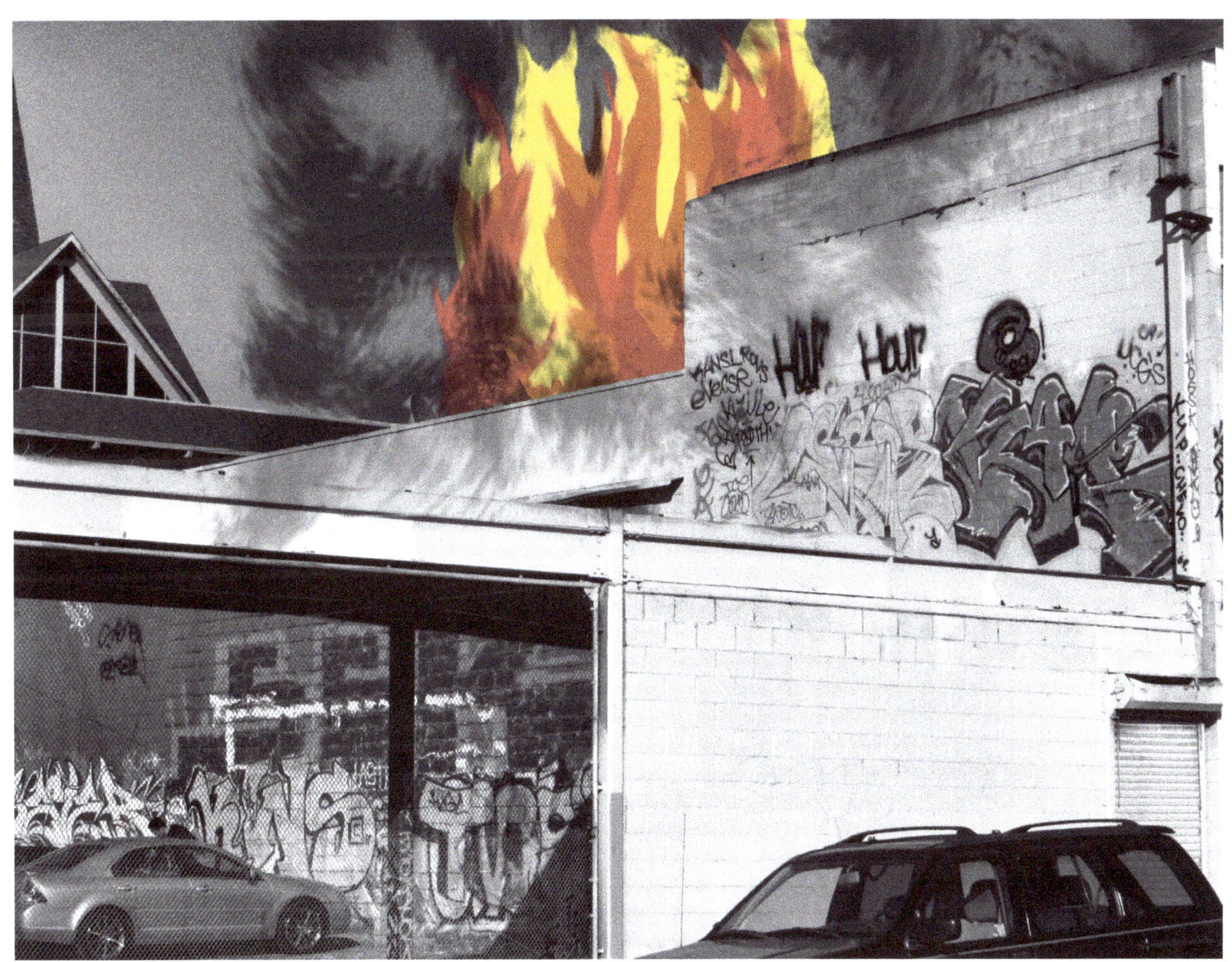

Burn; *digital illustration*, Luis Antonio Pichardo

Inside Story
(a play)

Tina Fallon

While their parents are away in San Diego visiting family, Carmen and Jamie, two sisters, are forced to stay inside their South Central Los Angeles house after seeing reports on the news of violence and looting.

Carmen, 18, is rereading the same book.

Jamie, 12, is cutting out pictures from a magazine.

Jamie:	(*Mumbles.*) I want a soda.
Carmen:	What?
Jamie:	Nothing...
	(*Pause.*)
Carmen:	I heard you say something.
Jamie:	No.
Carmen:	Yes, I did.
Jamie:	Well...
Carmen:	Yes?
Jamie:	Forget it... just forget it.
	(*Long pause.*)
Carmen:	(*Softly.*) Don't lie.

Jamie: I… did say something.

(*Pause.*)

Carmen: Then what is it?

Jamie: I… It was nothing, I told you!

Carmen: You can tell me!

Jamie: You won't want to hear it.

Carmen: Yes! Why not?

Jamie: BECAUSE!

Carmen: Oh come on, just tell me!

Jamie: I want a soda!

Carmen: NO!

Jamie: But…?

Carmen: You. Know. Why!

(*Pause. Jamie puts head down.*)

Jamie: You said I can tell you…

Carmen: Anything but that. We can't…

Jamie: I know, I know… I just want…

(*Carmen looking out of the window down stage left.*)

Carmen: So do I.

Jamie: Then!

Carmen: It is too dangerous.

Jamie: My friends and their family have gone out and nothing happened to them!

Carmen: I don't care, there are too many freaks running around.

Jamie: Carmen, it's safe now.

Carmen: I'm not ready, we can't risk it.

Jamie: I'm not scared, we can carry a big bat for protection!

Carmen: Jamie, they killed Mr. Beckett!

(*Silence.*)

Jamie: I… I know, but…

Carmen: I can't. I can't go out there anymore. There are people who are not… there are people who just don't care about human beings. They are angry! I don't want to see it.

Jamie: But we are not like them!

Carmen: (Crying) Mr. Beckett…

Jamie: I don't know why… I don't know why he was killed.

Carmen: I do! Because of hate! And the crazy people are allowed the freedom to run amok! There's not enough cops! People taking their kids to the grocery store while they… just take whatever they want? This is not the world I ever expected to live in! Innocent people getting killed and beat in the street! What's going to happen if someone tries to harm us? Who's going to help? Who in authority? There's no one to trust. There is no one left.

Jamie: Carmen, I'll be here. I will stay here with you. Maybe one day…
But today, I will stay here with you.

(*Carmen walks to the door and opens it.*)

Carmen: Do you still want a soda? You should go out and get it.
Maybe you could bring me one, too?

End.

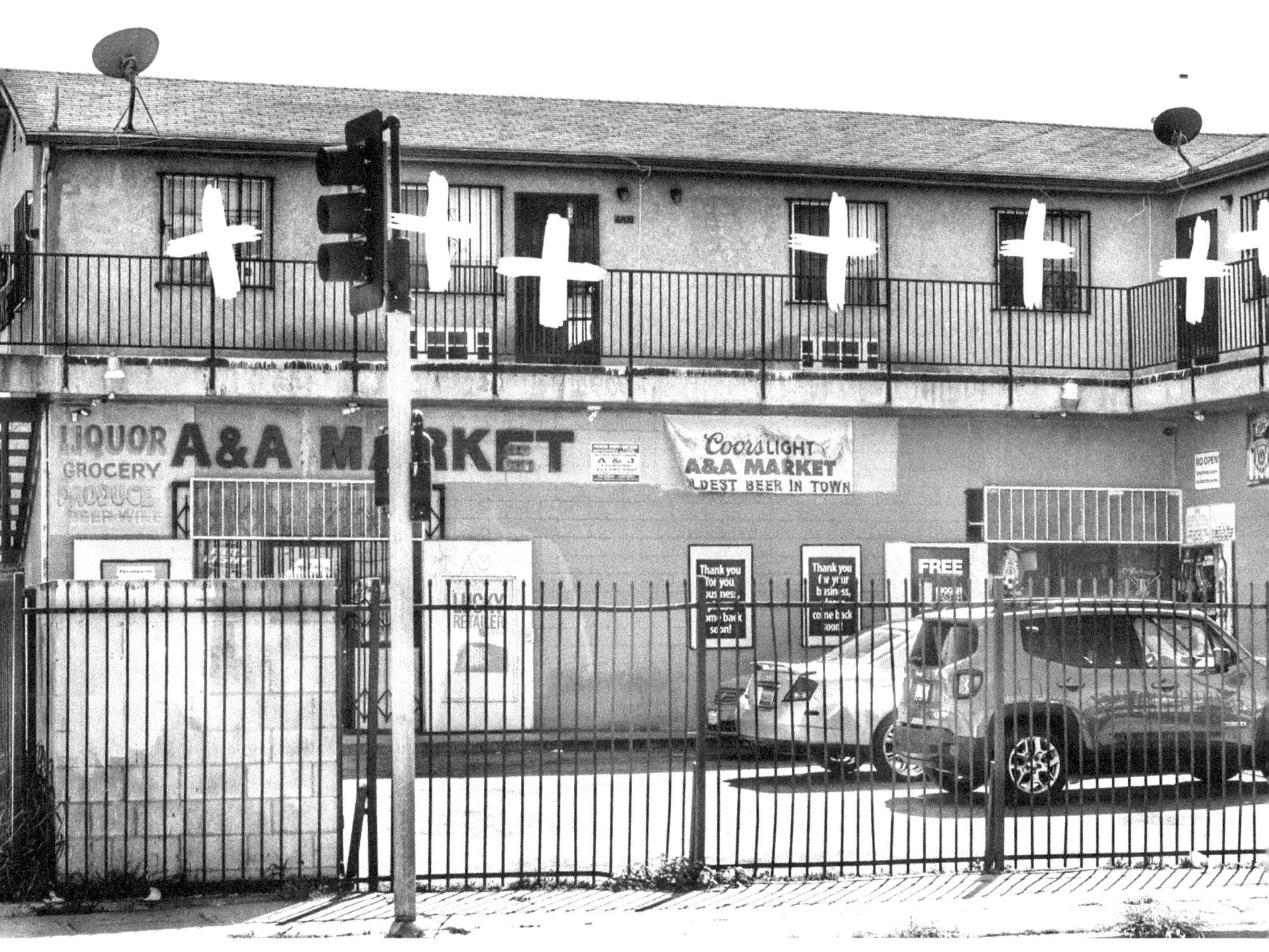

Housing/Liquor; *digital illustration*, Luis Antonio Pichardo

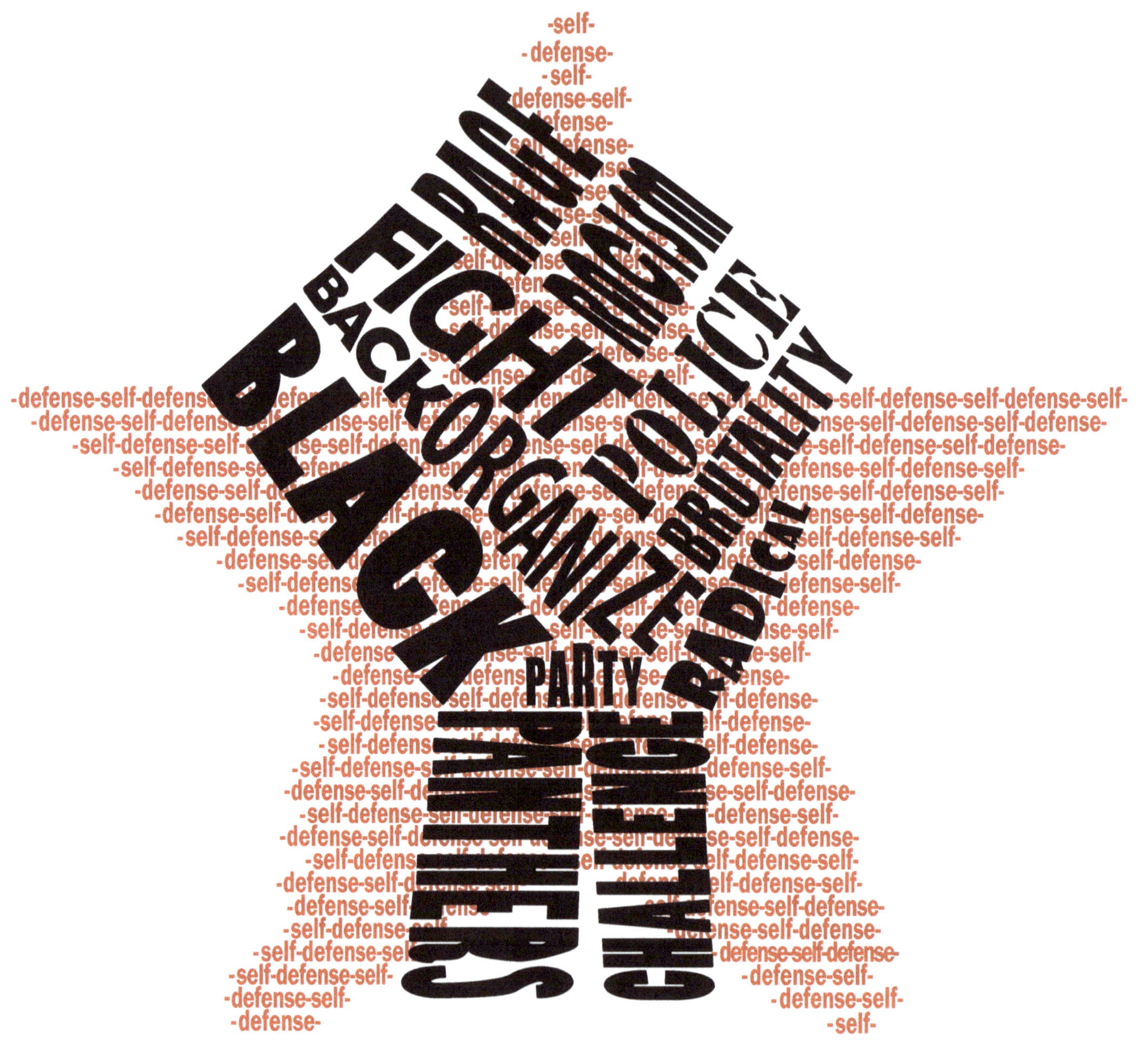

Black Panthers; *digital illustration*, Abraham Jaramillo

We Were Not Taught Vital Truth In School

Mello "Bluez" Houston

we had to piece together bits & pieces of broken knowledge
& mostly fend for our young selves. the boys admired
the gangster stars like Capone or anybody
actor James Cagney portrayed...
girls were not really instructed how to protect
their future motherhood roles. colored women
of science math genius were not even mentioned...
we were taught how to be grateful Lincoln freed "slaves"
meanwhile we all were "slaves to difficult economies,"
maybe today too. fortunately in the musical days of JB,
The Godfather of Soul we had us a real "Funky President"
of "soul power" beats uplifting much self esteem.
Enter the flashy 1980s
an island girl performer named Grace. Sister Jones sang
"Slave To the Rhythm" danced her narrative
of survival back amidst a carnival zone...
thereby many colored girls
& boys found ways back home
cosmic hand-made poems
Riffs o' Rhythmic Sound...
we were not taught many things directly
even now one has to dig for truth to seek
new birth* dancing to the old melodies
while loving this "bitter earth."

2-Part Essay

Michelle Smith

These dates are in the Month of March: an Aquamarine dream and sea of blue and the flower of sweet pea. Birthstone and Birth flower. My Grandmother Evelyn would have been 105 on the 28th, and my former husband, and six-year-old son's father, turned 66 on the 25th. History and Ancestry of a river runs through it. And what is it? On March 3, the ghost of a shell from racism, oppression, cultural indifference when Latasha Harlin's execution over a bottle of orange juice resulted in voluntary manslaughter, and in March, 13 days later, Rodney King endured a beat down by four who are to protect and serve, he was the martyr whose violence was a shot heard around the world. Our people, struggle and the Injustice. As In the savagery of Emmett Till, Rodney King was beaten within an inch of his life. He, a scapegoat for his plight, was used as an example of what Coon, King, Wind, and Briseno almost got away with, and what King endured. Thank God for the videographer, for a picture speaks 1000 words, volumes, and years. There was no right with this wrong. From Wednesday, April 29, 1992, 25 years later, have we truly over come?

In coincidence, Dr. Martin Luther King, valiant in his "Over the Mountain Top" speech, was assassinated the next afternoon. Rodney died of drugs and alcohol, and died in a swimming pool. Racism has won pre-, during-, and post-Obama. We of the black race American or foreign born continue to experience trauma. I thank you Rodney, Martin, and Latasha, for CAAM, and I have not forgotten how racism has a vice grip and is polluted and poisonous, and so are we as black mambas.

Broken Signal Lights

Abraham Jaramillo

"Hands on your steering wheel, where I can see them."

"Do you know why I stopped you?"

"A difference in our skin pigments has made me the OTHER; and social and economic stereotypes have made me a prime suspect of a collective paranoia, so,

Officer, yes, I do know why you stopped me."

"So, let's peacefully agree that my signal light is once more, BROKEN..."

Monsters Wear Blue

Luis Antonio Pichardo

Not royal; navy.
Dark navy, practically
black. And a brass shield.

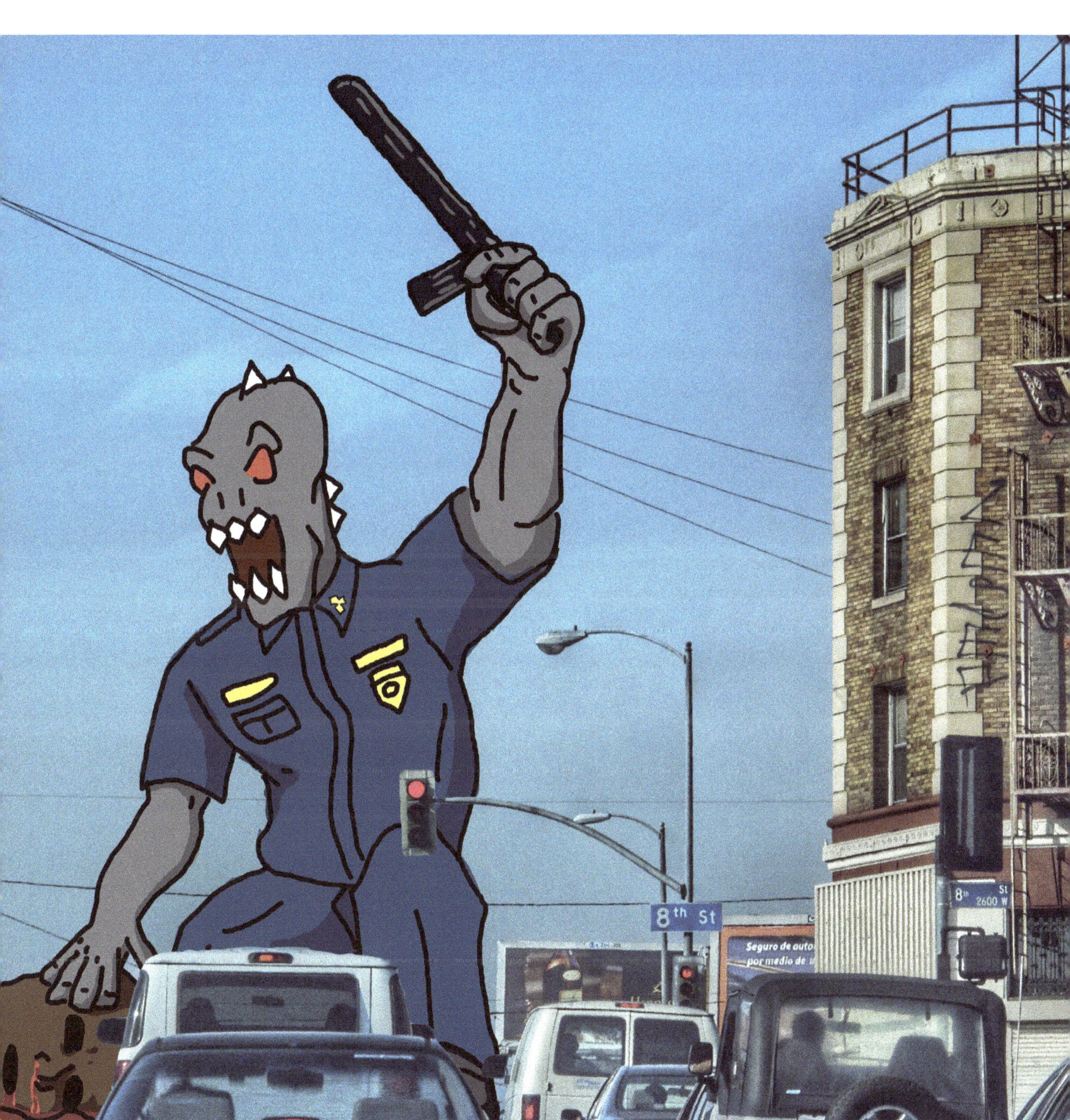

Monsters Wear Blue; *digital illustration*, Luis Antonio Pichardo

The Verdict

Maggie Kane

"Did you hear?" she exclaimed.
It is almost three.
I am in the library.

"The verdict is in."
I ask, "What do you mean?
What is happening?"

"They were acquitted!"
"The trial in Simi Valley?"
"Yes, the cops are free."

How, why?
Rule of law?
Must be some flaw.

I am afraid.
What to do?
This is all new.

Martial law in the streets.
Chaos, fires, smells.
Buildings burnt out, dead shells.

Times are tough.
Los Angeles, city of hope.
Riots; unable to cope.

Yet, we recovered,
From this awful dream.
Or so it seems.

Ice Cream

Jennifer C. Fuentes

Antonio loves ice cream. He's been in love with ice cream since he was a little boy. Early on he discovered that ice cream was his best friend when no one else was there for him.

It was there when his parents fought.

When he was bullied at school.

When he struggled with algebra.

When he was bored.

He didn't share ice cream with anyone. Ice cream was his only best friend.

He would hide behind the washer and dryer to eat his ice cream. Ice cream and Antonio became so close that ice cream never left his body. It saturated his every being, making him expand. Now, in the 7th grade, ice cream had been Antonio's only friend. He was lonely.

One day, Antonio's city, Los Angeles, went crazy, and people started to go into stores and took everything they could. Antonio had never seen so many people out on the street except during holiday shopping. He watched as people ran out of a store with stolen stuff.

Antonio ran into a Thrifty's Drug Store. While in the store, people took all they could. Some laughed, some brought big bags and put things in them. "Why do you need all that?" Antonio asked. But he was pushed and shoved, until he saw his best friend. He ran to a big freezer where Rocky Road, Pistachio, Dark Cherry, Rainbow Sherbet and many more lived. He began to stack tubs of ice cream on top of each other.

With a shaky tower in his hands he ran out of the store and jay-ran across the street. On the way, Antonio dropped half of his ice cream tubs on the street. Looters ran to the ice cream and took it all.

Antonio sat on the curb with the only ice cream tub he was able to steal. People took over the streets, but Antonio didn't care. All he wanted was a spoon. He took a deep breath when a strange, toothless lady sat next to him. She smiled and patted his back. "You are going to be okay."

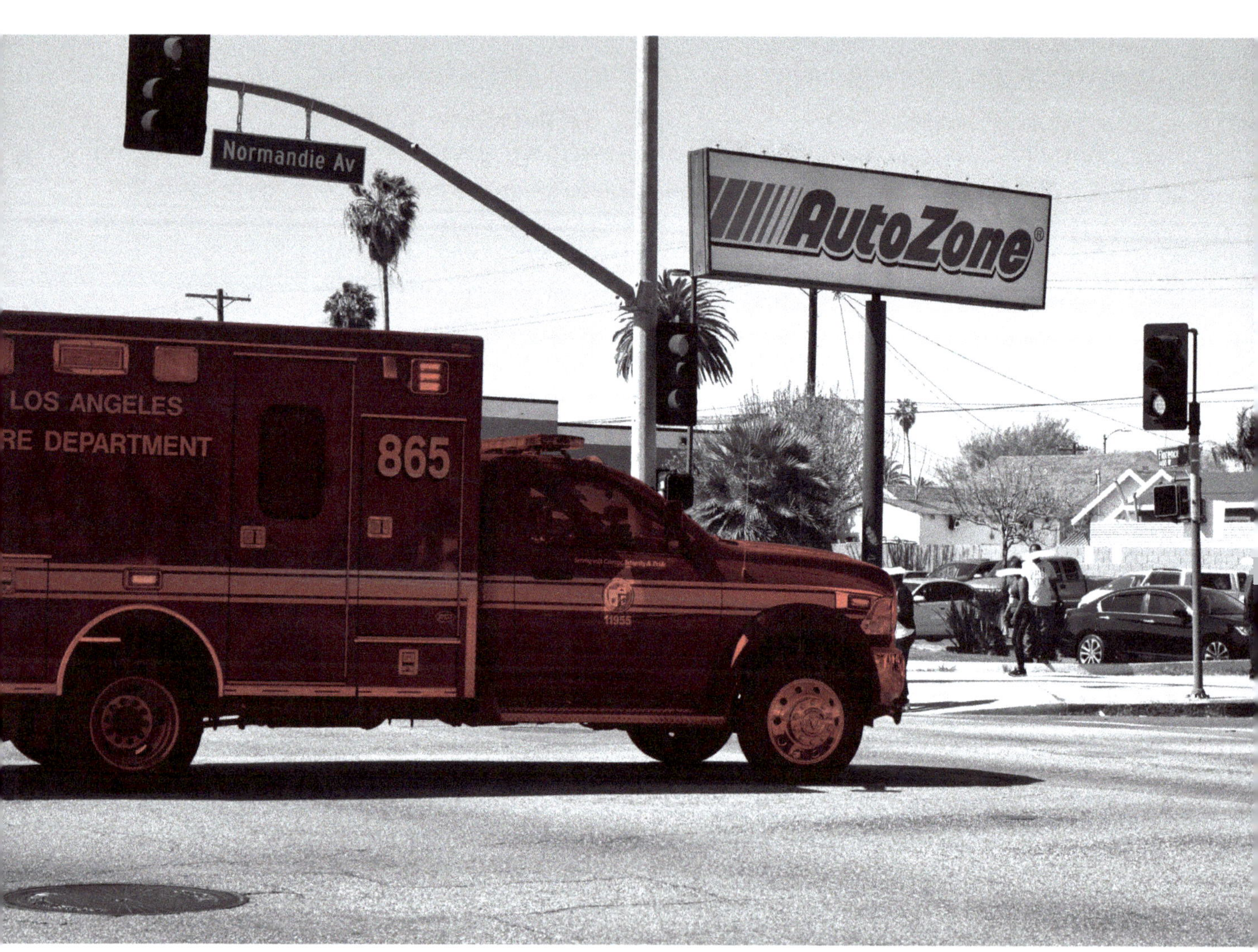

Normandie; *digital illustration*, Luis Antonio Pichardo

Waiting for the RTD

Christian Valles

As I witnessed a big box shoe store burned on Vermont Avenue and Santa Monica Boulevard from a wheelchair waiting for a RTD bus, it was late once again. Early in the year, I had reconstructive surgery on my feet. Functioning on my feet became diminished within months, words were my only savior against the world. Several disenfranchised families from the neighborhood, were waiting for an opportunity to gain shoes for the school year. The shoes were manufactured in a foreign land, while bootlegged Jordans, which their feet occupied, purchased in an indoor swap meet, began to fall apart from the seams. Desperation brought the family to gain scraps from civil unrest, fleeing from a nation scorned by civil wars, and economic oppression. In the end, the smoke will clear, the structure will be left in ruins, only to remembered by a few.

Out of the Ashes

David Fallon

out of the ashes
crawl lives torn to bits
covered with detritus of hate
zombified men and women
souls etched with violence
hearts bleeding with fear
that comes from war
a battle brought by desperation
a battle fought in throes of subjugation
that represents a stammering nation

out of the ashes
stream memories that will last into eternity
scenes of buildings burning into the sky
of innocents dead in the street
storefronts smashed and gutted
a legacy of loss
flowing like sour, cheap wine
down the throats of victims who want to forget

what are the things we will say
when we stop to remember this day?
what songs will children sing
about the rights and wrongs
a day like this inevitably brings?
will they speak of four heroes
who saved a beaten truck driver from certain death?
the woman who sat beside him
refusing to back down

the man who took the wheel
to drive him from that town
the lady in the car in front
who bravely lead the way
the man who hung on tight
to keep away the fray
will they tell of other heroes
who saved the homes and lives of neighbors
at the risk of their own lives?

out of the ashes
we learn much more than history books
can teach
much more than clergyman
can preach
we discover what it means
to be human
feel the power of the wrath of anger
in the face of injustice
we see destruction
inflicted by impoverished hands
who have been pushed to the brink of doom
it is a warning to us all
we always reap what we sow

out of the ashes
the spark comes alive
to push back when oppressed
to protect and save the innocent
to give ourselves for betterment of others
to make the world a better place

out of ashes

the new will always grow

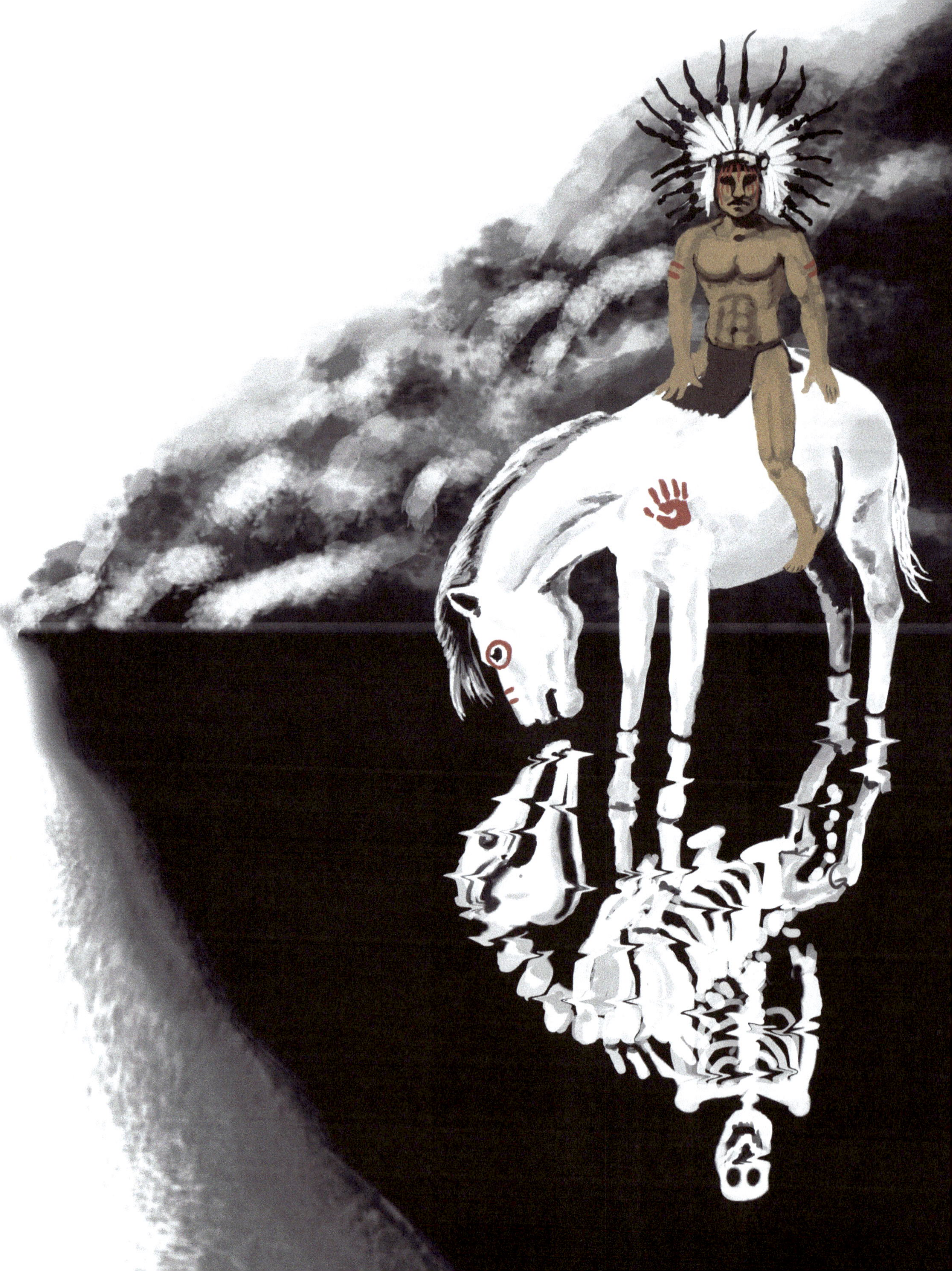

On Day 6—Recovery

Maggie Kane

We recovered from the city riots.
Day by Day.
6 days of finding a way.

From groups and loyal citizens,
businesses and local communities.
They reached out, created unities.

Some of the ideas and solutions
became manifestations
of community innovations.

"Rodney King," L.A. Riots, a generation ago.
What has been remembered since 25 years?
Yes, Los Angeles has many fears and tears,
but I am still here.

Indian Warrior; *digital illustration*, Abraham Jaramillo

Brick

Luis Antonio Pichardo

Brick, scent of
cocoa butter and blood
stains, grains, pores,
the chores of carrying
weight, burden, witness
to fires, both gun and
flames, you weigh
a man down with shelter.

Brick, scent of
silent bakeries burning
industrial aluminum, nonstick
trays and browning buns,
dulce sabor de saber
that furnaces burn dreams
and you hold them in
flukes of ash and cinder
spewing American hopes
skyward as bricks fly
into crashing screens.

Brick, scent of
electronic discharge, kinetic
vapor of police beatings
caught on tape, Black Lives Matter
so much as a baton matters
crashing into my
skull, your skull, our
skull, and bricks

berate riot gear because
fear keeps you planted
along Wilshire and San Vicente.

Brick, scent of
Korean blood, White blood,
Mexican blood, sweet
and sour belief that Black
blood is purest
and must be taken.

I resent you brick.

Why do you have
the color of me?

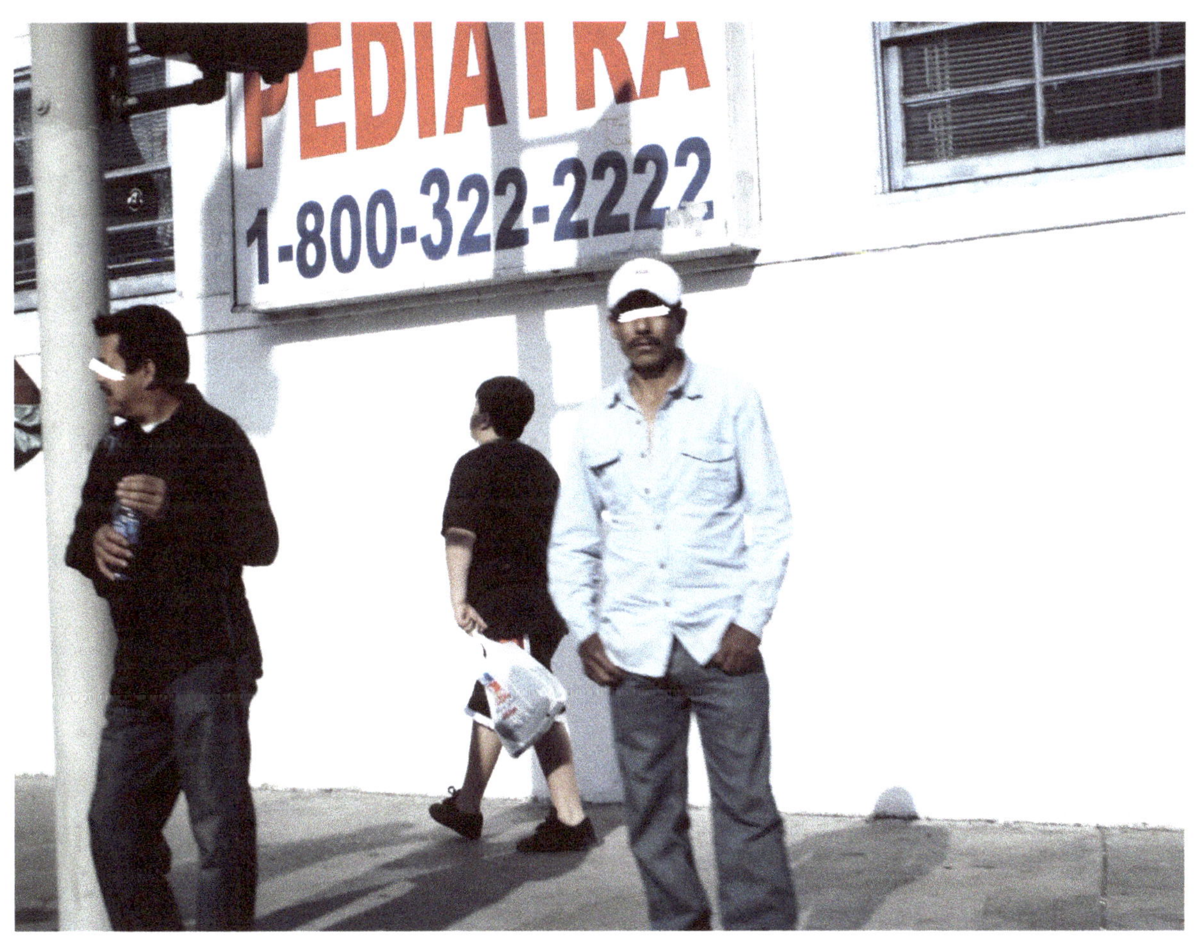

Bystanders; *digital illustration*, Luis Antonio Pichardo

El Diamante

Jennifer C. Fuentes

At three in the morning, one Summer morning, two sisters, Rosa and Santos, were driving on the 10 Freeway East in a food truck on their way to work when a drunk twenty-something collided into them head on. The truck flipped and rolled across the freeway. Pots, pans, spices and hot cooking oil shifted from side to side with Santos, the cook in the back, while Rosa, the driver, ate some glass.

Both sisters recovered and received $10,000 in a settlement as a result of the accident. It was Santos who finally decided to do away with the man that was exploiting them, the owner of the food truck, and invest in a restaurant. She assured Rosa she would never go back to this man and that she was now finally ready to start fresh with someone who actually loved her.

"How about it Rosa? A restaurant!"

"We don't know anything about owning a restaurant."

"We both know food, and everyone eats."

Rosa was not sure. She initially left her job at the sweat shop to work with Santos because the owner of the food truck didn't always pay her her wages. Rosa had always come to the rescue, and decided to drive the food truck when the man who previously drove it suffered a heart attack and couldn't work anymore. Rosa drove while Santos cooked. Rosa stood up to the factory-worker perverts on their route who harassed Santos. Rosa was also there every payday Friday to threaten and demand their weekly wages from the owner. It had been this way since they were little girls. Rosa, the big sister, came to the rescue when Santos was bullied. Rosa was getting tired of it all.

"This time things will be different, because this time, we will be our own bosses. I promise," Santos plead.

Rosa was uncertain about the whole thing. On the one hand, she would be able to keep a close eye on her younger sister, but that also meant she would now never able to escape her nagging, stubborn and vulnerable ways. But she would also make sure Santos was always respected and got a paycheck. That also meant Santos would never be able to care for herself.

Rosa visited a psychic that assured her it was the right decision and that they would both be successful. Soon enough, the two sisters were signing papers for the cockroach-infested El Diamante Restaurant on Manchester Blvd.

A fake blonde by the name of Socorro, who Santos knew from a friend of a friend's cousin, sold the restaurant to the sisters. Socorro said that the only reason she was selling the place was because her mom was ill.

"I wish I didn't have to," she said while pouring runny refried beans into a Styrofoam container, "but my mom is alone."

Socorro always spoke while playing with her hair. Although Rosa doubted Socorro's honesty, and was intimidated by the iron barrier that separated the cash register and customers, the trauma of going back to the food truck was unbearable. More than anything, she wanted Santos to be happy. Socorro happily took the $10,000 check from the sisters, although she was originally asking for double that.

The sisters did not know the first thing about owning a restaurant. They were ignorant of how to attain a food-handling license, and were unaware that an arrogant health inspector with a silk scarf would be popping her head in unexpectedly. They didn't know what a business plan was, nor researched the population they were going to serve, or their competitors. They had no menu. But then again, they didn't even know the kind of food they would be selling.

The sisters jumped in a deep body of water without the ability to swim, without a life jacket. They imagined a grand opening with lines of people who by magic knew instinctively they needed their food. Santos, specifically, imagined counting thousands of dollars at the end of the day, imagined taking her kids out of their shitty schools, saw herself and her kids in a spacious house in the suburbs, and imagined eventually paying someone to run the restaurant for them. It was going to be the best investment ever. But first, they had to get rid of the cockroach problem.

Rosa invested in an Executive Costco Business Membership and bought packs of Raid to begin with. Santos hated Costco. She once complained that she hated the smell of cardboard and plastic, the crowds, and the fact that she once ate an entire oversized bag of spinach that was going to expire, only to make her sick. Rosa made her a ginger peppermint tea then. Santos now walked around Costco, grumbling, trying not to hit people with her shopping cart, picking things up and tossing them back.

"How necessary is it to sell two pack pints of tapioca pudding?"

Rosa learned to block out her sister by humming.

"Are you listening to me, Rosa?"

"You wanted a restaurant, didn't you? This is where restaurant owners shop!" And she put a yellow, industrial mop strainer in the cart.

They spent the first few days cleaning. Socorro left a mess. The more they cleaned and sprayed, the more cockroaches appeared. The place reeked of ammonia, bleach and poison. They scrubbed, dusted, scraped sang and cussed. They painted the inside of the restaurant. Rosa wanted a clean and practical white, but Santos suggested pink since it was her favorite color.

"A light, powdery pink would be nice."

Rosa rolled her eyes.

"That's a nice woman's touch you got there," a homeless man said who peeked his head in. "I like pink myself."

In the three weeks that the sisters prepared El Diamante, only a few people walked by. Foot traffic was sparse. The homeless man who liked pink might have been one of the few who walked by the restaurant daily. Everyday he complimented the pink walls, asked for change, and walked away. One day, after having stocked the restaurant, Santos gave the homeless man a Coke.

"This is a business, Santos! You can't give things away," Rosa scolded.

"You have no heart!"

• • • •

The sisters tried to change the restaurant's name to something else. On their way to City Hall, Santos made a list of names she liked: Santos's Kitchen, Santos's and Rosa's Kitchen, Delicious, Good Food, etc. Rosa drove and agreed that Rosa and Santos's Kitchen was the best choice.

They entered the building and a stoic woman with a bad haircut and clumpy mascara told them the process was long, might cost them thousands of dollars, depending on whether they had a lawyer or not. She was bored and tapped her pen on her desk: "Anything else?"

The sisters made grand opening flyers and reluctantly settled with El Diamante as the name of their restaurant. Santos told the man who made the flyers to include illustrations of diamonds on the flyers without Rosa knowing. Rosa found the illustrations tacky and tasteless. She was constantly irritated now. She hoped people only looked at the grand opening date,

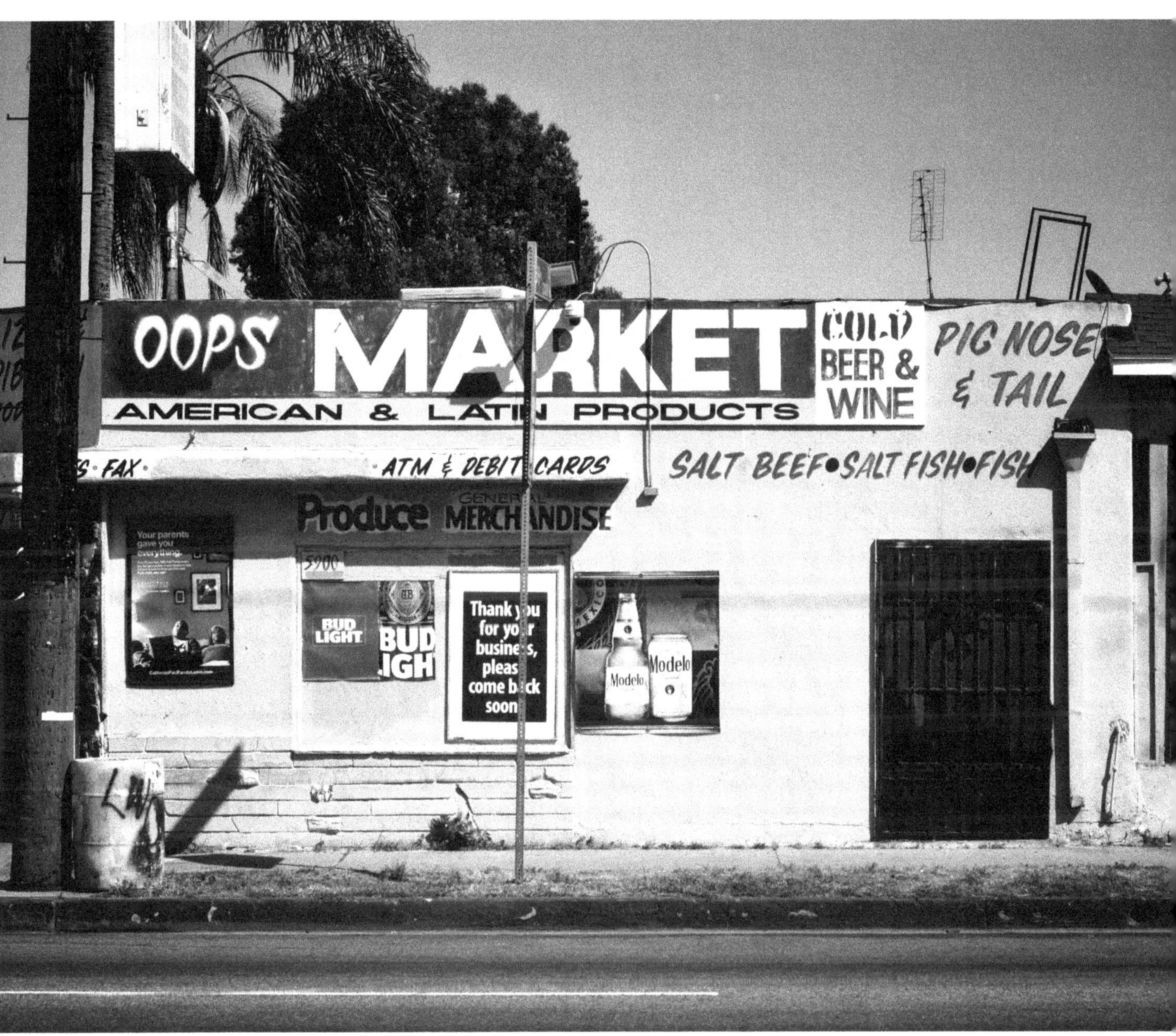

Oops Market; *photograph*, Luis Antonio Pichardo

March 1st, and their weekday Enchilada and Cheeseburger specials.

All the orange, blue and green flyers that scattered the neighborhood made no difference, because El Diamante remained empty for days. For days, Santos stirred hot, canned nacho cheese that never bathed tortilla chips. After two days, she threw away the refried beans and rice to make a fresh batch only to throw it away again after a few days. Santos and Rosa became tired of eating rice and beans, stale tortilla chips and the other left over food that didn't sell. And when the one rare customer walked in, Rosa and Santos practically rolled out the red carpet. They offered samples, extra salsa, extra fries and more of everything. Rosa constantly asked if everything was okay, if there was anything else she could bring, and she would stare at the customer from behind the iron barrier to observe any gestures that would indicate the customer was satisfied.

"Thank you, come again, please tell your friends we're open!" she would say to customers on their way out. They never complimented the food, or the service, or anything.

And on these rare occasions, Santos would taste her food and claim that maybe her food was too salty, or too bland, or just not good enough. "Maybe the neighborhood knows Socorro sold the place, or maybe he saw a cockroach," she'd say. "Rosa..."

But Rosa was already watering her lucky rue and lighting her gold candles to attract money.

By the end of the month, El Diamante had a few regular customers. It took some time for the next door neighbors, owners of a tire shop that had been there for generations, to discover that El Diamante was open for business. The owner was an older black woman in her 70's that came to work everyday, although her children and grandchildren ran the tire shop smoothly. The lady always ended her sentences with "honey." "Thank you, honey; you smell lovely today, honey; how much was that, honey?" She wore fuchsia blush and beige nylons with the nylon vein never straight on the back of her calf. She smelled of cinnamon and orange poppies, and for some reason, loved Rosa's 7th grade daughter's handwriting.

"Look how lovely you write, honey?"

One day, Rosa's daughter was writing an essay while eating a bean and cheese burrito. The essay was in response to Rudyard Kipling's story "Rikki Tikki Tavi" and Rikki's heroic qualities. Although the 7th grader was inarticulately attempting to summarize the story to the tire shop owner, whose name no one at El Diamante ever learned, she was more interested in the kids writing.

"You know, my husband's writing was so similar to your writing, honey. Before he died, he wrote me a letter and it looks like your writing there, honey." She took a napkin from the dispenser on the table and wiped her tears.

"What did the letter say?"

Rosa gave her daughter a look while cleaning a table, indicating that she shouldn't have asked that.

"That he loved me, that he's always loved me, and to be kind, he was always a lot kinder than me, honey."

She took her to-go order of enchiladas, her usual, from Santos through the little window in the iron barrier. "Smells great, honey, better than Socorro's." She tipped Santos, Rosa and Rosa's daughter, and walked out.

Other regulars included a man who wore clothes with dry paint stains, a lazy eye and a bald head, who never looked at the menu or specials. He would take out change from his pocket and ask Rosa what he could buy with that. Rosa barely looked at his hand and always responded with chips and salsa. And Santos would always add a little something, some fries or onion rings in the bag, when Rosa wasn't looking.

There was the Guatemalan Christian couple who never left without a prayer for El Diamante. They would raise their arms to the air, sway their hips from side to side and shout out God's Eternal Glory into the ammonia-infested air. They rejoiced as soon as they took a bite out of Santos's torta de chicharrón, dark-red chicharrón sauce dripping over their light colored church clothes. They would mumble something under their breath when Rosa charged them more for extra salsa or avocado slices, and made sure to remind her that her plants and candles were the devil's work.

And of course, there was the regular customer who could not recover from her good friend Socorro's departure. Concha would walk in wearing stretchy yoga pants and a t-shirt two sizes too small with a sequined logo that read "Sexy and Loving it." Concha would complain about the blandness of Santos's rice, how salty her french fries were, and how she should have just asked Socorro for her recipes.

"Why do you come then?" Rosa said once from behind the iron barrier.

"Customer is always right," said Concha.

"You're not!" Rosa was ready to escort her out.

"You know, I wouldn't get rid of this iron thing. Socorro almost got killed. Didn't she tell you? Some kid once took all her money with a gun."

"Just leave, Concha." Rosa gave her her salty fries in a Styrofoam container.

Santos looked at her sister in despair.

• • • •

Among all these characters was a narrow, tall woman with a mushroom haircut who

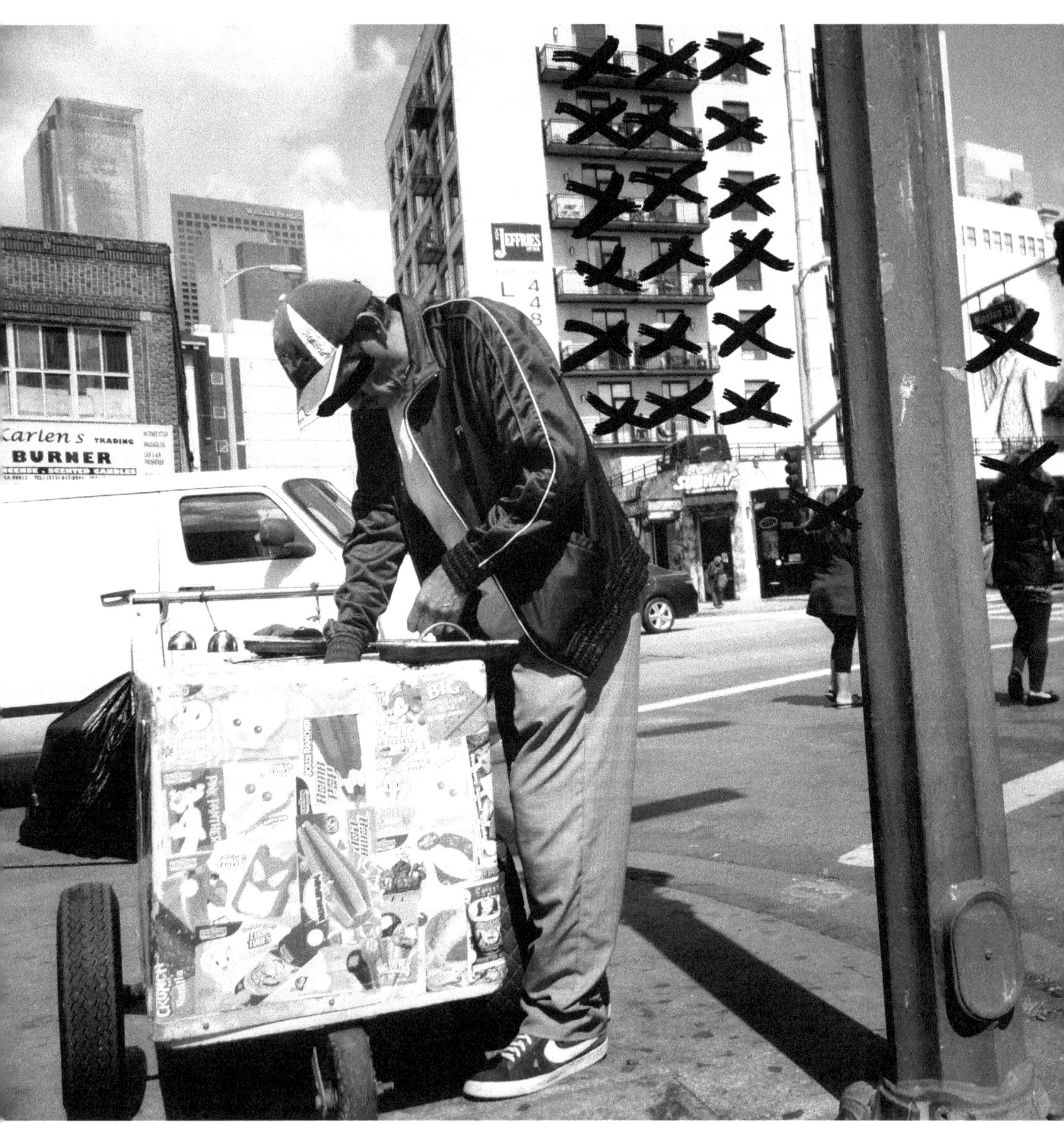

El Jale; *digital illustration*, Luis Antonio Pichardo

wore a silk, flower print scarf. She was a woman of a few words, and was El Diamante's assigned health inspector. She made little to no eye contact, and had little, sharp, pointy teeth. In two months, this woman visited El Diamante six times, and every time, nailed Rosa and Santos for something. She'd walk about with a clipboard; it would be so silent that they could only hear her heels, the scribble of her pen and their hearts. Rosa was the one that usually followed her and asked questions as she herself wrote down notes on a napkin. She was always too nervous and scatterbrained to find a notebook or a piece of paper to take notes on. Rosa would nod and smile and oh yes, oh I didn't know that, oh yes, we'll take care of that right away until the mushroom left. The health inspector would downgrade them for not having a meat thermometer that worked, on not having an up-to-date exterminator report, although she never saw a cockroach or any other uninvited insect, and once for finding Rosa's half-eaten cheeseburger near the sink. On one of those occasions she charged them $100.00 for a re-inspection, and in the end, Rosa and Santos received a C for a grade. Rosa was certain that the big, red C they had to shamefully hang in the front window was what kept customers away.

"I wouldn't worry about that, honey. Just give people good food and treat them good, and they'll come, honey. Trust me, honey," the tire shop owner said.

• • • •

The days continued, and business was slow and steady, long and exhausting. Rosa and Santos bickered some days about stupid and petty things, and on others days they worked in awkward silence. Some days they joked and remembered when their father was around. It was on one of these days that Rosa told Santos for the first time that she'd promised him she would take care of her. Santos said she already knew this.

Some days, no one walked in until noon, and other days, one of the usuals was waiting outside for some breakfast and coffee. Some days there was but one or two customers, and other days, it was so busy that Rosa's husband had to go to the market and buy extra everything. The days were unpredictable. Rosa believed that Concha had something to do with why business was not consistently busy. She did, after all, find a picture of both her and Santos under a tree surrounded by egg shells and human excrement. The tire shop owner assured Rosa that Concha was harmless.

"She was the same with Socorro, honey. Just treat her like any other customer and she'll eventually back off, no need to fret over someone who's just plain lonely, try to have some compassion, honey."

Rosa rolled her eyes.

Days later, on a Wednesday afternoon in late April, while Rosa and Santos were sitting around figuring out new lunch specials, the owner of the tire shop walked in, out of breath.

"You must leave and close this restaurant now, there's a riot not too far from here, honeys."

Rosa and Santos were confused. It was still bright outside, a little past six in the afternoon. It was too early to close.

"It's at the corner of Florence and Normandie, honey. And some poor man got taken out of his truck and beaten, I think he might be dead, honey! Mercy me, please leave now, and don't take that route home, honey. My kids and I are leaving now, honey." And she wiped her sweat mustache with a napkin.

It was at that moment that Rosa's daughter called, telling her of the incident. She also pleaded that they close the restaurant and come home.

Rosa's knees began to shake. She closed her eyes and saw a wave of rioters making their way over on to Manchester Blvd., a plague that would destroy everything they've worked so hard for. She quietly recited a short prayer and began storing and packing food to take with them. Santos moved quietly and efficiently. Santos knew better not to say much when her sister was this way. Santos followed suit, called her kids, and told them she would be home early.

"I'm going to meet you in the car, Santos. Don't forget to lock up, turn the lights and everything else off. I don't know when we'll be back." Rosa took a deep breath and walked out.

The homeless man who liked pink walls was sitting on a few loose bricks outside. He looked up at Rosa. For the first time she noticed his eyes. They were bright. She realized she liked him. She gave him the food she had packed to take home and some of her tips.

"I hope to see you soon," she said.

Santos did the sign of the cross, took her sisters rue, left the lights on and locked their restaurant.

It took longer to get home that day. They avoided surface streets to get back home to Pico Union and took the 110 North instead. On the radio, they heard that Reginald Denny, the man who was driving a semi-truck didn't know he was driving into a riot and was almost killed, but thanks to a couple who saw the incident on TV, Denny survived. Santos covered her mouth and gasped as Rosa drove in her beat up Ford station wagon. They learned that the riot was a result of the acquittal of the four white LAPD officers who beat a black man by the name of Rodney King a year ago.

"So the officers are free?" asked Santos.

"Yes."

"Do you think we'll be able to open tomorrow?"

"Santos, let's worry about getting you home first before things get worse."

"Things will get worse, they have to," said Santos.

• • • •

The sisters did not see each other the following week. They lived fifteen minutes from each other, Santos living in East Los Angeles, but a risky fifteen minutes since the rioters had taken over the inner city; shops everywhere were looted and burned to the ground. The image of Reginald Denny on TV almost beaten to death traumatized Santos so much that she didn't even think of leaving her apartment until the coast was clear. She and her kids ate nothing but canned garbanzos and Chocolate de la Abuelita for the next six days.

Rosa's situation was a lot worse. Her quadruplex in Pico Union that was only surrounded by businesses was almost burned to the ground, if it had not been for her husband and the neighbors who climbed onto the roof with garden hoses. Everyday for the next six days, Rosa called the owner of the tire shop for any possible updates, but not once did she answer. Rosa threw up most of these days.

After six days, when the riots had subsided, Rosa, Rosa's daughter and Santos made their way to El Diamante. They traveled down Normandie Ave. Los Angeles was not the same city. From the back seat, Rosa's daughter made a list of the places that were no longer existent or altered. The wall that surrounded the cemetery on Normandie was defaced with graffiti; some parts of the wall were broken piles of dirt and dust. The dead must have awakened and broken the wall, Rosa's daughter thought. Rosa's botanica where she would occasionally get her palm read was now a small, empty and dark lot where a botanica would never again exist. Rosa's laundromat that she would only visit to wash her husband's dirty work rags was partly there, half of the place destroyed. The owner swept outside as if he was opening for business.

Most liquor stores closer to South L.A.— gone. Wig shops, bargain fashion stores— gone. Restaurants, fancy or not— gone. The streets were mostly empty. The melancholy was deep; so much deeper than taking out a splinter from an index finger with a tweezer. No, this here gloom was rooted, deep down, and firmly in a city that was tired of the same old thing. Most of El Diamante's daily customers were a reflection of this: people who, although worked hard, tried their best, and were people of faith, they had a hard time simply living. They were also tired of it all. They were all South Los Angeles residents that could have, also, easily have been the target of the four acquitted LAPD officers.

Rosa had to stop to occasionally throw up. Santos quietly sobbed. Rosa's daughter stopped writing as they approached El Diamante and rubbed her aunt's shoulders. Rosa's bottom lip quivered. She held her sisters hand, parked the car a few blocks away and prayed. She loved her sister more than ever.

They could not see anything but ashes as they approached.

"I think its gone," Rosa said in a broken voice.

"No, it's not! Look!" said Rosa's daughter.

When they got closer, they saw that El Diamante stood strong, confident, and firm among the stench of destruction and defeat on Manchester Blvd. with a huge sign in the window that read "Black Owned" in handwriting that looked all too familiar to Rosa's daughter.

"I can't believe it. Rosa, look!"

"I'm looking, Santos."

The three of them sat quietly in the old Ford Escort, the adrenaline still shaking their bodies.

"Santos, didn't I tell you to turn the lights off?"

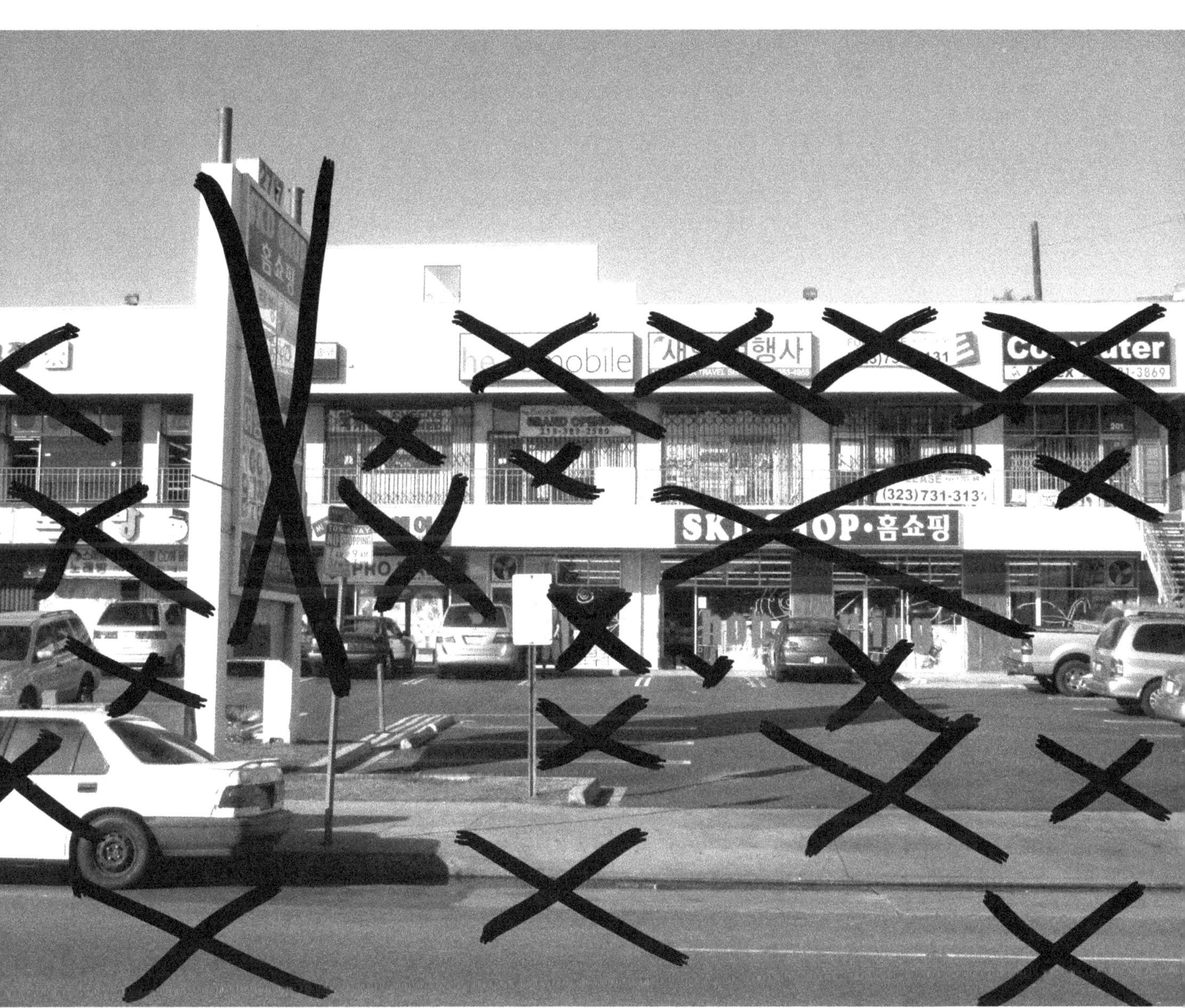

Shutdown K-Town; *digital illustration*, Luis Antonio Pichardo

Restricted

Tina Fallon

IN Los Angeles
the homeless
are OUT
on sidewalks
and pressed against
the underpass
they plant their roots IN
condemned buildings
at the forefront
of store fronts
and schools
closed for the day
searching for space
not requiring rent.

No place else
I am bothered
there are certain agreements
accordance with the law

Here you can
there you can NOT
Over yonder between
the hours of such and or such
You can but only
where it is not restricted.

Re
STRICT
Ed

As in, His parents are 'strict'
the homeless were once a BABY
or
That teacher is 'strict.'
What happened to the homeless in school?
Was there school?
Wasn't there a class or
        maybe a unit on, How Not To Be Homeless.
We are humans
Who migrated to be
IN.

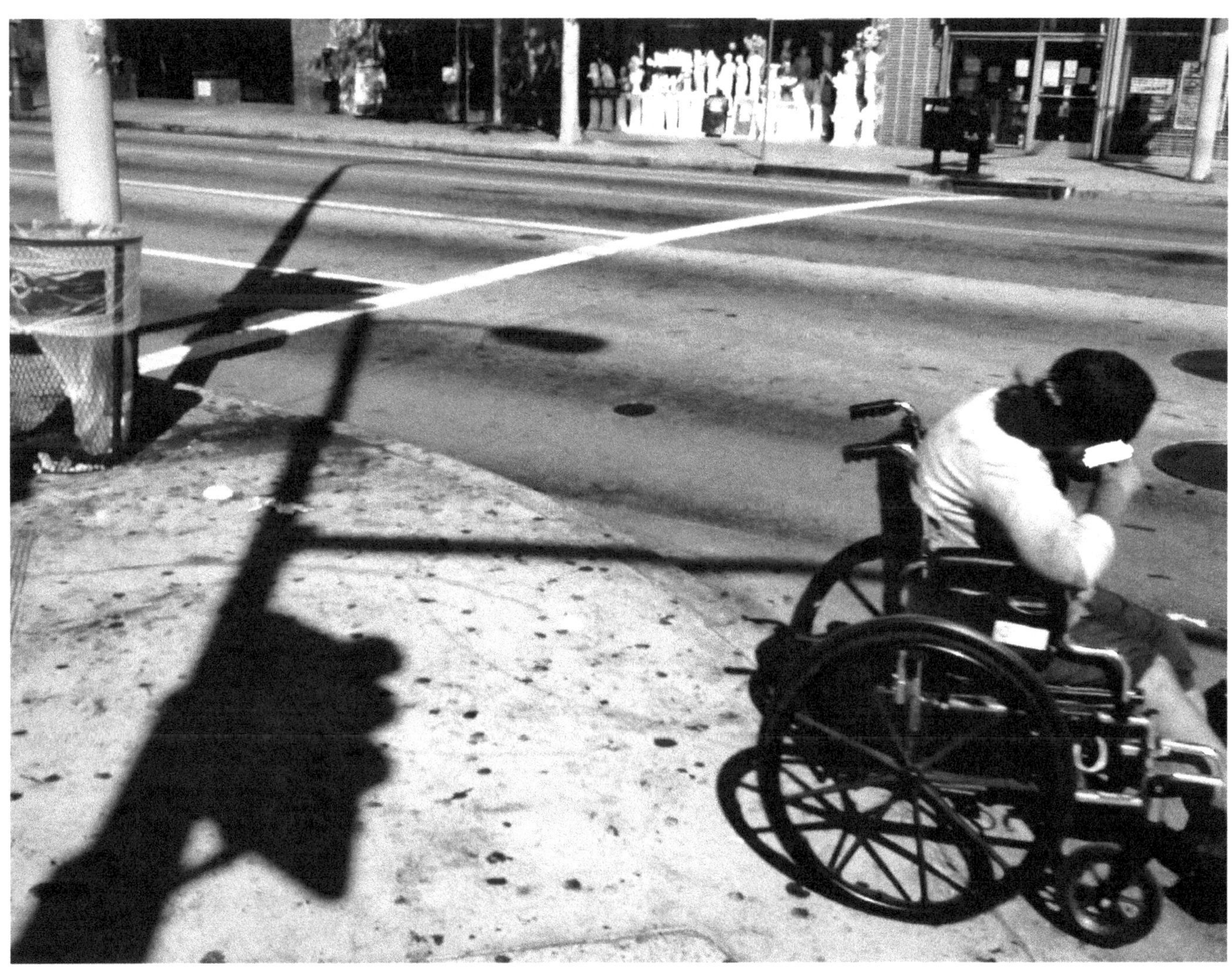

Sin Rumbo; *digital illustration*, Luis Antonio Pichardo

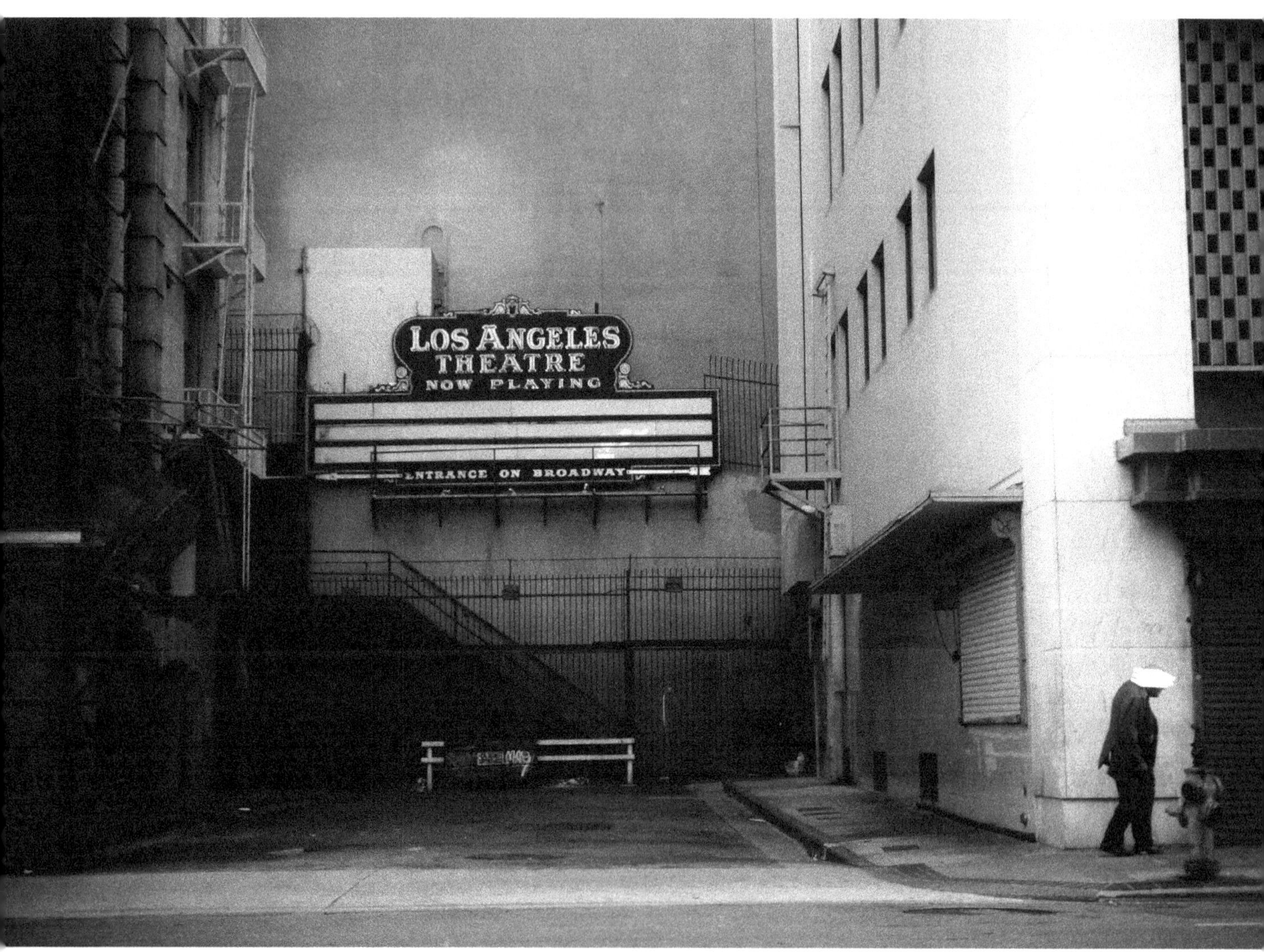

Theatre; *digital illustration*, Luis Antonio Pichardo

When Josephine Baker Waz Homeless in France

Mello "Bluez" Houston

When Dancer, Josephine Baker: Homeless In France...
When Writer, Zora N. Hurston Forgotten in a Poor Hospital.
When Sly Stone was Homeless on Slauson In his Camper
When Issac Hayes was Sleeping on Dionne Warwick's Sofa.
When Bob Marley: Poor Sleeping On Rita's Mom's Kitchen Floor
When Many "Hollywood Swinger's"
Dreams Fall Apart On Sunset
And Tents Go Up In Venice Beach, Skidrow, Crenshaw, Anywhere...
Then they can sing that blues song,
"NOBODY KNOWS U WHEN U DOWN & OUT."
And Find Out What Struggling Is All About...

......my great aunt's home was taken by the big banks in 2009...

First 100 Days of Mr. Trumpff

Susan Chavez

There's going to be a change
because there's been a healing.
Social justice Warriors
have been aligning themselves
across all the components that affect
the political, social, ethnic and religious issue-rights
that are being symptomatically compromised
during these first 100 days.

We are healing because we are taking action.
We are talking, organizing, analyzing and strategizing
to correct those practices that
are being attempted and coerced by Mr Trumpff.
We are warriors
we come from an ancestral lineage
that is fiercely dedicated
to the lives and well being
of our families especially our children.

We have collectively come together through our thoughts,

Women's March #4; *photograph*, Abraham Jaramillo

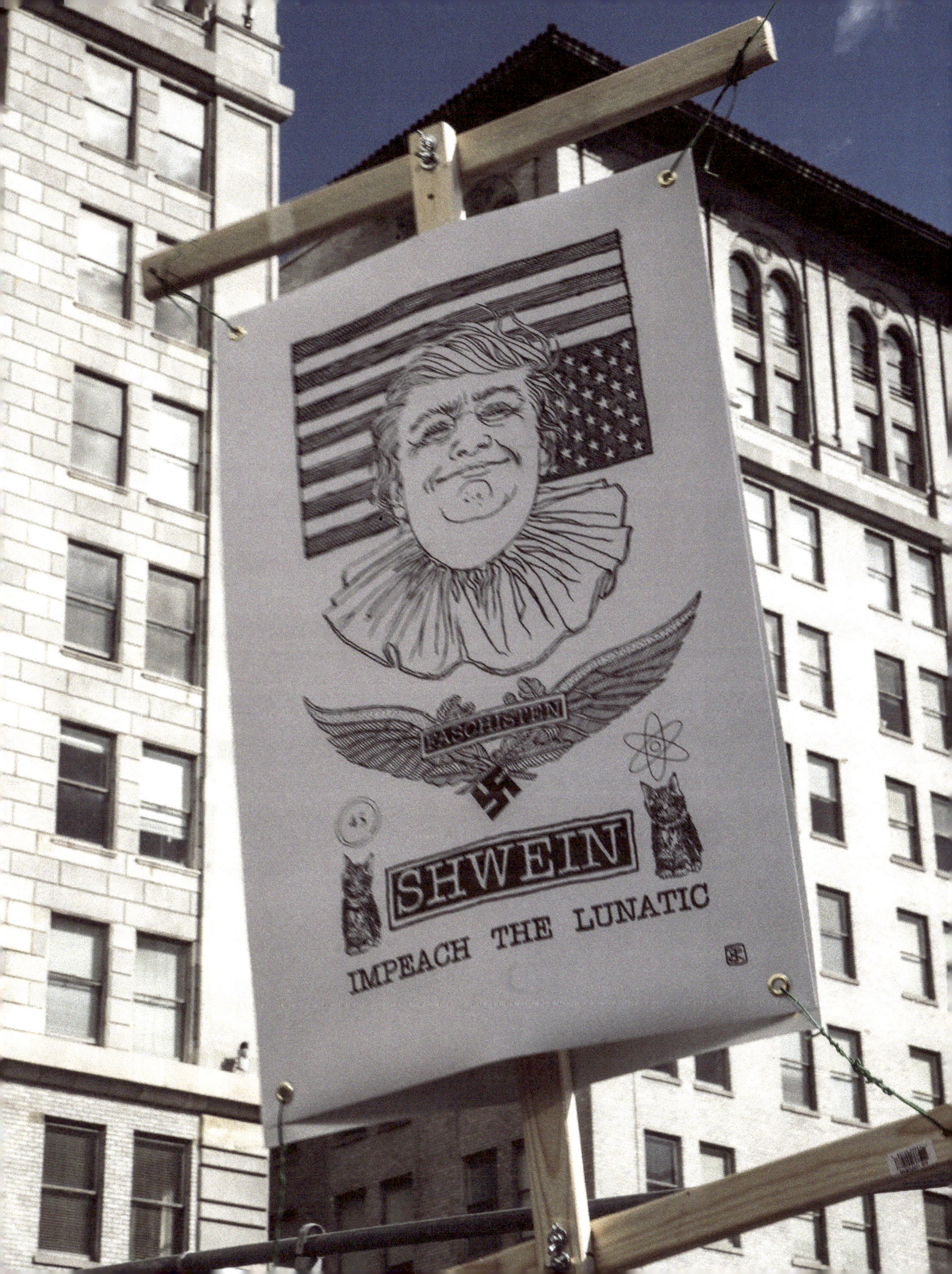
FASCHISTEN
SHWEIN
IMPEACH THE LUNATIC

but first we came together through our hearts
and first before that, through our minds.
And ultimately the original source
we all share in common
is that we all come from the same essence.
So together it's been possible
for us to collectively work
as we have for these first 100 Days.

Even at a distance,
from the Atlantic shore to the Pacific shore
we each are united.
We are from the same tribe.
We share values.
We speak justice,
we speak concern.
And this is what's happening all across the United States.
I feel that, and I know that.

Amen

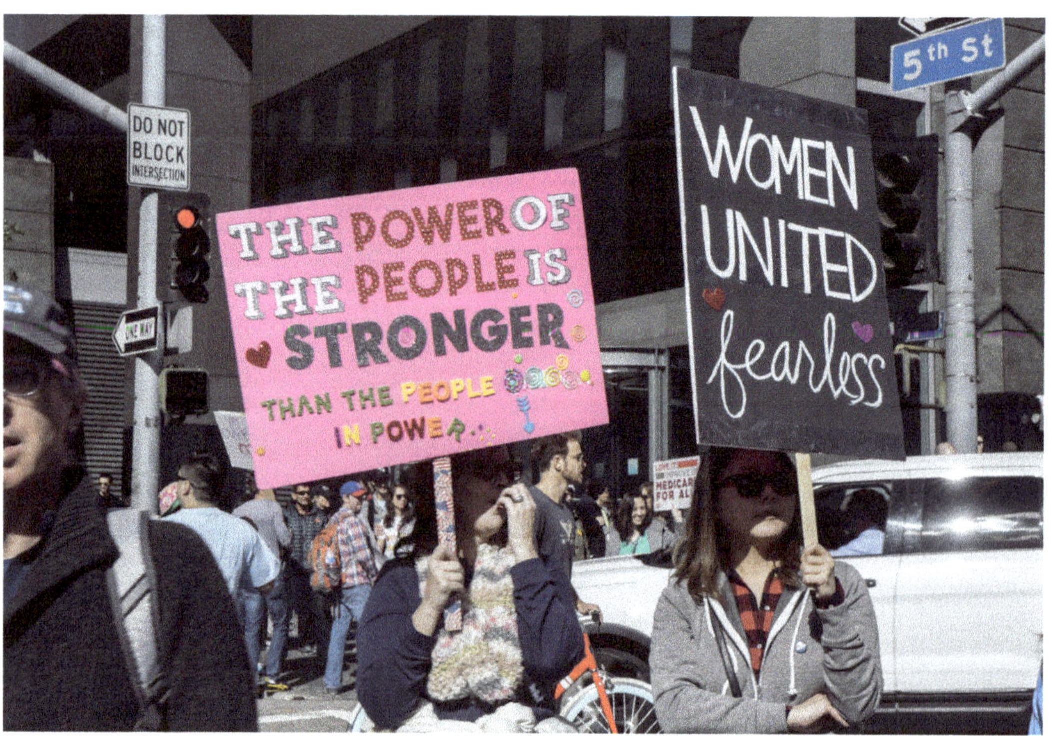

Women's March #9; *photograph*, Abraham Jaramillo

1992

David Fallon

In 1992, I was a sophomore in college at Cal Poly Pomona where I was studying theatre arts. I sort of stumbled into this major by accident, joining a few high friends one Summer to audition for a local community theatre. The play we acted in was a typical family comedy with bratty kids who get their comeuppance at the hands of their much wiser parents. Based on this experience, I was not convinced that theatre was the subject for me. That was until I took classes where we read the works of the great masters: Samuel Beckett and his utterly unique theatre of the absurd filled with disillusioned characters who joke in the face of their bleak existence, David Mamet and his ultra realism portraying angry characters in search of personal redemption, Edward Albee and his angst-ridden worlds of humanistic conflict, and Bertolt Brecht and his grand Epic Theatre which was politically charged and screaming for social change. I was hooked, and though I did not know it at the time, this was the beginning of a life-long pursuit of high art, philosophy, and words of ultimate meaning.

That Spring, I was disappointed to find I would not be cast in the main stage production of Beckett's "Waiting for Godot", a play about two downtrodden men who desperately awaited the arrival of a mysterious figure named Godot. The plight of these men alternates between moments of hopefulness and hopeless with lines such as: "In an instant all will vanish and we'll be alone once more, in the midst of nothingness!" The director told me he thought I could play the lead but he had decided to put women in the roles instead. I worked on the props for the play and spent an inordinate amount of time driving to thrift stores in search of things like luggage, pipes, and spectacles. I watched rehearsals from the sidelines and dreamed about the day I would put on my own production of "Godot."

Indeed my focus had begun to switch from acting to directing. In between classes, I was working on an adaptation of a little known play by an all but forgotten playwright. Georg Buchner died of typhus in 1837 at the age of 23. He left behind only 3 plays, the most famous of which was found unfinished and in fragments. "Woyzeck," based on a true story, is about a put upon man who is driven to madness by the various oppressive forces in his life. In his break with reality, he ends up killing his girlfriend who has cheated on him with a younger, stronger man. Since the play was discovered in a fragmented state, it is up to the director to decide how to structure the play. I spent hours that spring reading the scenes in different orders to see what insight it might bring to me. I read tortured lines like: "Try raising someone like me on morals alone. Man is flesh and blood." I pictured Woyzeck the lost soul grappling with the forces of the world against him, forces that seemed hellbent on his destruction.

At the same time, we were studying the works of Brecht who was an advocate for the poor that spoke openly and bravely about the injustices committed by institutions like the Catholic Church. In his play, "The Life of Galileo," he criticizes the church for subjugating one of history's greatest thinkers. He illustrates the lengths the church will go to protect its precious doctrine, that it will not hesitate to ruin the life of Galileo in order to stop the progress of science and free-thought. "Mother Courage and Her Children" is about a 17th century mother who follows an army during the 30 Years War. She does so in order to sell provisions to the soldiers, the money of which she uses to care for her children. Sadly, in a realistic portrayal of the consequences of war, one by one her precious children become collateral damage. It was Brecht who once wrote in appeal to the humanity of us all: "First feed the face, then talk right or wrong."

So it was the end of April 1992, while under the influence of these writers, that the L.A. riots unfolded into my life. Because of the breadth of my studies, I did not really have time to watch TV. I would go to school as soon as I woke up in the morning, attend classes during the day, hang out with friends in the afternoon, and participate in theatre production in the evening. I usually did not get home until after 11 PM. Then it was time to scramble through any homework before collapsing into bed. Consequently, I was unaware of the developments downtown. The morning of Thursday, April 30th, started out like any other as I prepared for the school day ahead, but that ended quickly when I drove up to the parking lot to find no cars and a security guard standing by. As long as I live, I will never forget the scene.

"Campus is closed," he stated gruffly.

"Really? Why?" I said in naive shock.

"You don't know?" he said with raised eyebrows. "You need to go home and watch TV. Now."

In the moment, it seemed like the oddest thing he could tell me. The trip back home was ominous. It became clear something serious was going on when I saw boarded up shops along Holt Blvd. and Garey Ave. When I finally got home to turn the TV on, the riots were on every channel. What I did not know at the time was that things were not only happening in Los Angeles proper, but things were going down in my very own home town.

In the next city over, about 200 mostly students from the Claremont colleges were marching down Indian Hill Blvd. into Pomona. They were acting in protest of the Rodney King verdict. Protesters chanted slogans like "Hey hey, ho ho, police brutality has got to go!" Later in the day, a peace rally was held at Pomona First Baptist Church a little over a mile from our home. Clergymen denounced the verdict and called for an end to the violence. When evening fell, groups of young men gathered around the Indian Hill Mall, which was a defunct shopping mall turned swap meet. They had been urged to meet by a flier calling for violent action. As soon as it was dark, such actions erupted. Rocks were thrown at cars, businesses looted, buildings lit on fire. The police, who were not at full strength due to officers being deployed to Los Angeles, refused to enter the fray. It is estimated that the mob numbered about 500 people at its height. While the destruction was nowhere near the extent of Los Angeles, it was nonetheless significant for the owners and residents involved. Some business owners armed themselves and did not hesitate to fire on the rabble. Police were dispatched from surrounding cities. They were eventually able to contain the crowd and it all ended as abruptly as it started.

The next day, no one in Pomona left their homes. A state of emergency had been called and the national guard roamed the streets. When it was finally over a few days later, there was a pervasive sense of shock, and no one quite knew what to say or think. Part of me was the rebellious youth who silently cheered at the thought of disenfranchised people getting much needed vengeance. Another part was the empathetic future-therapist who cringed at the sight of innocent people being hurt, innocent people losing everything. Still, another part of me was disgusted by the entire affair. Why did such things happen in a self-proclaimed "civilized society?" Why had the police taken it open themselves to lawlessly beat a defenseless man? Why had a jury of so-called peers come back with such a senseless verdict? Why did so many people feel the need to enact violence against their fellow man? Why did I live in a country that inspired such hate and suffering? Sadly, to this very day, the question remains: Why do I live in a country that inspires such hate and suffering? There are no easy answers, only more questions.

Soon after the LA Riots (as they came to be called), I wrote my first play which was eventually performed at Cal Poly Pomona. It was an examination of our fractured, meandering society. Written in poetic form, it explored subjects like poverty, environmentalism, homophobia, sexism, and racism. Characteristic of my young adult angst, there were harsh images, such as rape and murder. Characteristic of my young adult idealism, it was partly a plea to take action to make the world a better place. In the vein of playwrights like Brecht, I wrote: "When all is said and done/ Ours is not to question why/ We all are doomed to die/ And what will you have done?" To this very day, I continue to ask myself this same question: "What will you have done?"

Riot

Luis Antonio Pichardo

Diabetic legs shuffle,
pre-diabetic run,
cases of water,
testing strips,
a canister of O_2,
fuck it,
some gauze and
bandage wraps for
stimulating you, blood
flow, circulation
and smoke filling
lungs.

Gardner's hands,
gamer's hands,
burn at touch
of flame and cinder
blocks on fire
and cuts of meat,
sausage, chicken breasts
fill grocery carts, leave
veggies and freezer aisle
as they burn, Molotov.

Hit the register first,
baseball bat,
hockey mask, Jason
on the prowl tonight
with argonauts in tow

looting foreign hands,
lands of ancestors and
blood relatives,
mezcal and vodka bottles
burst as consumed
both in flame and rage,

we're killing pigs tonight.

Mover's backs
and spinal columns
universal carry burden
of couches and bedroom sets
made in Korea, China,
anywhere but U.S., jobs
and benefits of dreams
run out like sweat
amongst burning tires
and smashed gas cans,
fuming, evaporating
into oxygen-less air.

At least the baby
is sleeping
in it's own bed tonight.

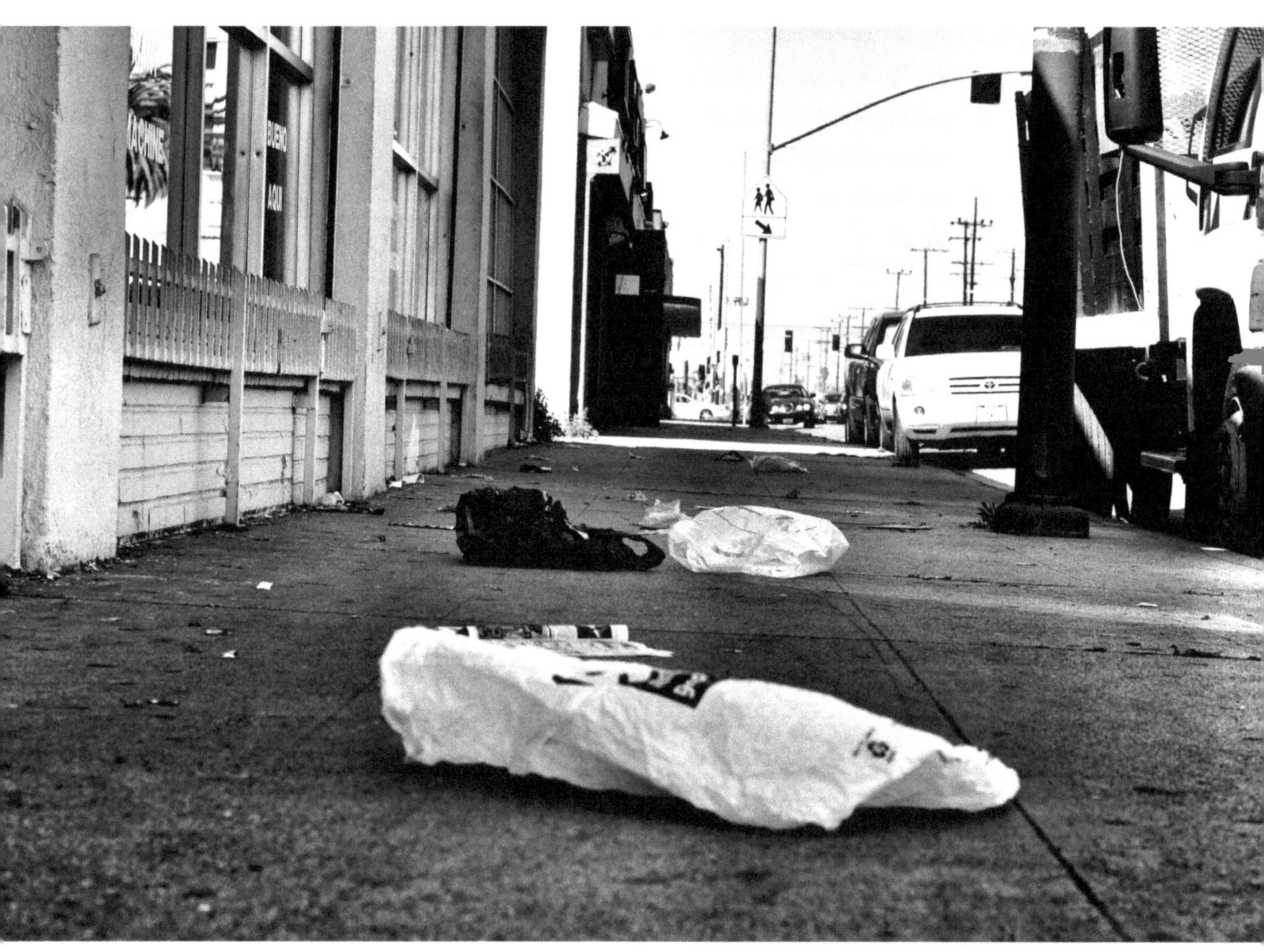

Litter(ed); *photograph*, Luis Antonio Pichardo

1992
(a poem)

Christian Valles

I.

It began with a denial of truth, even when the truth is presented in a modern visual of communication. Transported in an easy-to-open packaging to be consumed even by diabetic grandparents. As backyard parties attendants are consumed by cumbias, Morrissey, and wine coolers. As 40 oz. of malt liquors bring out the inner demons of young urban warriors. Tales of treason continue to be uncorroborated among the urban warriors, who find the answer in spraying ammunition to their enemies indiscriminately. While others repent to Christ but continue to be staying heavy.

II.

As the looters beat working class bystanders and burn the small capitalist attempts, my father escaped from the riots in a discolored Camaro with broken headlights. The Camaro: a demonstration of his wealth and triumph as an immigrant in the United States. The rest of the day was consumed in a distant neighborhood judging the looters through the lens of mass media. Only in the end, devouring stolen goods from car trunks; supporting the hood economy.

III.

Tonight we consume, what was denied to us in our homeland, success through determination and decision. Many of us can't remember God on Friday or Saturday nights after consuming 40 oz. of fiscal liberty. Only in the morning when their fiscal decisions become realities with lifetime consequences. The freedoms constructed by the marginalized natives are also enjoyed by the recent economic and social refugees. Thank you.

Brick

Michelle Smith

rick
        ick
                        ck
A heart of stone
Is shaped like a brick
Not concrete
But
Hard and rough
Just the same as love, life, and history
Can be
Savvy, strong, and experienced like me,
Yet beautiful
For it is part of a foundation,
And of color like me
My race
Wise and unique
As can be
Different shades and hues
From the Vanilla soul of Teena Marie to the Sun Goddess of Ramsey Lewis, Stormy Weather of Lena Horne, Billie "Lady Sings the Blues" Holiday, to the Blackberry of Nina Simone
There is more than Baskin Robbins and 31 Flavors

The VHS

Jennifer C. Fuentes

In 1986, my dad took our family to FedCo to buy the latest in technology—a VHS player. After months of saving a little bit from his hard earned money, my dad had finally saved exactly what he needed to buy us a VHS player, and maybe a movie to go with it.

"It's right here, mija, $679.00." He patted his pocket and smiled at me as I picked my Trix out of its pink milk.

"Is that a lot of money, dad?"

His smile shifted to a scowl. "Do you know how many brake jobs, oil changes, transmission overhauls I've had to do for this money? A lot! You kids don't know! And drink your milk! You don't want your bones to hurt like mine, do you?"

I didn't understand the connection between my bones hurting and nasty warm milk, but I knew better not to ask.

"So, will our VHS be better than Tio's?"

"Much better, mija!" His tone was upbeat again.

"Can we have more movies than them?"

"Don't push it!"

• • • •

We all walked into the electronics department at FedCo with a purpose. My mom didn't say her usual, "the sweet bread smells so warm and fresh, let's get a bag for tonight to have with coffee," and my five-year old little sister and I didn't run to the toy department. No. That day was no ordinary day. We knew how important this day was for my dad, so we never dared to show any other interest. Those were the rules. We knew better. But I didn't mind because I deeply loved everything my dad loved. So if my dad wanted a VHS player, then I wanted one too.

We were rich that day with $679.00 cash in my dad's pocket, ready to purchase what most people in our Pico Union neighborhood didn't own yet. A VHS player for my dad meant we had officially moved up in the world. It was what was needed to solidify our middle class status now that we had replaced white Wonder Bread for Oroweat whole-grain bread, and left Tang and Tampico behind for 100% Florida Tropicana orange juice. A VHS player was going to continue to elevate our family and add to my dad's fancy preference in Milano cookies instead of the Marilu's that were sold at the local, mice-infested Ranch Market. A VHS player was the perfect investment for this man, who unlike others in our neighborhood, desired an education so badly for himself, and now for his two daughters, that he so easily paid $400.00 on credit for a World Book Encyclopedia set from a door-to-door salesman. A VHS player made sense for the family whose children wore fancy hi-top Reebok's instead of the popular Pro-Wings-knock-offs that most of the other kids wore. This next investment was the most natural step for the man who would occasionally buy my mom a dress and a pair of earrings just because from The Causal Corner at the mall. This latest technology meant we were unlike those around us. A VHS player meant my dad and his family had "made it."

My dad and I both stood in front of the many kinds of VHS players. My mom and sister went to the movie section. My dad held my hand. It was warm. I looked up at him. His eyes glanced up and down, left to right, right to left. He let go of my hand, adjusted his glasses, and went straight to the player he wanted. The tag read $679.00. It was the highest number there, yet they all looked the same to me. He tried to take the thing out of its space but it was attached to a cord. He pulled it out as much as he could, looked at the back side of it, and ran his fingers through the outlets. He turned it to face him, and held it with both hands, looking at it straight in its face. The time blinked a red 12:00.

"I think this is the one."

I shook my head already day dreaming about watching Rocky V a million times over.

• • • •

That VHS player was the heart of my relationship with my dad. Friday night movie rentals from 20/20 video across the street from our pigeon-infested, run-down apartment became the thing that made me forget the fact that my dad was different from other parents. His vices were not typical of those of some of my classmates' parents. He was not an alcoholic for instance. He was not a womanizer like my uncles. But he was a narcissistic, self-centered man who did not have the ability to listen to anyone, no matter how rational or sound the advice was. He regurgitated and rambled, his words were always inarticulate and out of place whether he was in good spirits or angry. He usually spoke loudly, no matter the setting, and even when people managed to jump in and say a word or two, my dad finished their sentence. He was always on top, always the loudest, always the "wisest," always the most dominant, always the "best." Those that knew my dad well knew better, and they let

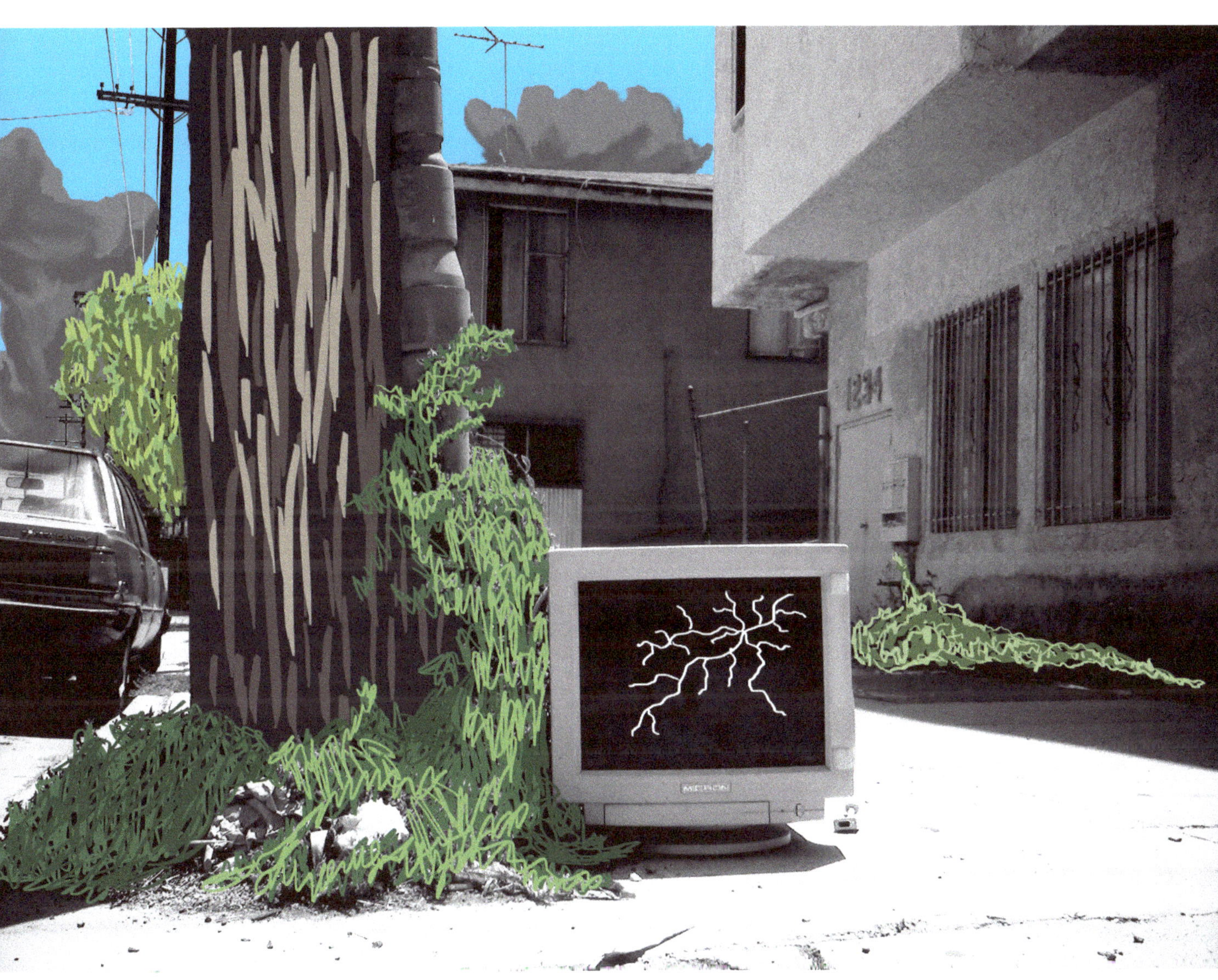

Obsolete (modified); *digital illustration*, Luis Antonio Pichardo

him talk while they daydreamed of what to have for dinner. Those that didn't know my dad endured the pain and struggled to say a few words here and there, finally giving up and either ending the whole incident with a sarcastic comment, or with laughter. These moments were the most difficult to watch and listen to. I used to hide in the closet and cover my ears. Sometimes I used to sing or hum loudly until my mom would tell me to stop being rude. Other times, during these disastrous encounters, I would sit on his lap, snuggle up, and dig my face near his armpit so that he may become distracted and give me the affection he thought I wanted. But all I really wanted was for him to stop talking.

The older I got, the more embarrassed I became. And the older he got, the louder and more irrational he became. It was difficult for me to understand my dad's need to always be right and to adapt to his extreme behaviors. One day, he became an enraged animal when, while playing, I accidentally broke a tusk off of one of my mom's collectible, porcelain elephants that he never even cared about. The very next day he mocked and ridiculed me in front of my friends for not knowing one of his stupid fun facts about cows. (He always spoke about cows and pigs because my grandpa was a butcher.) He laughed so much at me that day that the little pieces of popcorn he was eating were spilling out from his mouth. I was his entertainment that day. I remember wanting to run away while screaming everything out of my system that kept me alive. But I sat there and took it all in like I always did.

• • • •

But Friday nights were different. When the 2:30 bell rang on Fridays, I'd run out of Magnolia Elementary School's gates and find my dad waiting by the ice cream truck. He'd buy me an ice cream, wait for me to eat it before getting in his clean Toyota Camry, roughly wipe my hands clean, and we were on our way. On our way home, I'd tell him about the movies I wanted to rent that night, and he would remind me that we were only renting two, and that the weekend should be dedicated to homework, not movies, and on and on and on. He would ask me if I wanted to repeat a grade like my cousin, Danny, and even before I could respond, my dad would say he didn't want any dummies in his house. I knew the rule of two, but I always insisted, hoping one day he would budge without his lame lectures. Nevertheless, it was Friday and nothing really mattered.

At about 5:00pm we would make our way to 20/20 Video. Every week I wanted to be tough and jaywalk across the heavily-trafficked Vermont Boulevard. And every week, my dad scolded me about safety while we walked to the slow traffic light. Once we got to 20/20 Video, we'd split up. He always made his way to the Action section, while I went to the comedies. His choices usually consisted of anything with Chuck Norris, Arnold Schwarzenegger or Charles Bronson in it. And whatever I chose, whether it was Back to the Future, Bill and Ted's Excellent Adventure or Pee Wee's Big Adventure, he almost always made a comment like, "Really? Looks terrible, like there will be too much talking!" I never argued and smiled, knowing well he was going to rent it anyway.

He never allowed anyone to touch the VHS player. For years he had a faded-orange face towel on it where my mom would place her picture frames with photos of us next to her lucky, porcelain elephants. Every Friday my dad would take everything off the VHS player to put the cartridge in the player. And about once a week he would dust it. He went crazy one time when I saw the silhouette of a cockroach inside the VHS player, blocking the red, digital time display. "Cuca!" I yelled, and he ran into the living room to find me pointing straight at our movie player. He quickly took the towel off, set everything else aside, disconnected it, took it outside and shook it violently while rambling and cussing at the cockroach to get out. When that failed, he took a screwdriver, popped a little door open and out came the culprit. He stepped on it, continuously smashing it by rubbing his shoe from side to side into the floor, mumbling under his breath. My dad then cleaned the VHS player and put it back in its place gently, as though he were rocking a baby back to sleep.

On Friday nights, my dad did little worrying; little talking, if any. He didn't argue, he wasn't "right," and he didn't laugh at me. It was when he was the most happy too. At least it was when I was the most happy. We sat next to each other and watched movies. Usually, it was just my dad and me watching Chuck Norris dropkick his nemesis while I worked on a 1000 piece Christmas puzzle that I don't ever remember completing. My dad never said anything to me, sometimes he would sit on the floor and help me with the puzzle. Other times, we sat while he cracked my fingers or massaged my back. But most of the time, he watched closely and quietly. We'd watch both movies, his eyes almost shut by the end of the second. And almost without fail he'd say; "my movie was better." Then he'd go to sleep.

• • • •

By the time I was in middle school, the Los Angeles riots broke out. And my bonding with my dad over movies was still in full force. Up until that point, we had never missed a movie Friday. But on Thursday, April 30th, 1992, things changed, and they never really went back to normal after that. It was that day that I remember so clearly, because it was written largely and boldly with white chalk on the chalkboard in my 7th grade English class. I knew there would be no movie night the next day.

I knew we were in trouble because my tall and lanky teacher, Ms. Chung, who was generally never moved by anything, went into panic mode on April 30th. Never, until that point, had I seen her teeth. She usually nodded or shook her head, pointing at things. Our theory was that because she was married to our sweaty and scary math teacher, Mr. Chung, she must also have been traumatized by him. On April 30th, I learned that her teeth were pieces of yellow chiclets. She didn't know what to do with a class full of scared twelve-year-olds. Although the windows were closed, we could still smell the fires. She paced back and forth, looking out the window with the text book in her hands trying to read Riki Tiki Tavi to us. She refused to put on the news for us, claiming it was going to make things worse. We protested, but to no avail. I thought about my family. Where were my parents? How was my sister? Would I still have a movie night? And why the hell was I in school with this wound up woman? Luckily, right when I wanted to start tearing up, my mom showed up.

By the time we got home, my dad was at the balcony of our old apartment complex watching people trying to break into the 20/20 Video and the Thrifty's Drug Store. I stood next to him, again he held my hand. It was warm. He was quiet.

"Should we start packing, dad?"

I could hear my mom opening and slamming drawers and cabinets, zipping and unzipping bags.

"Let's get the VHS player," he said.

Manos; *photograph*, Luis Antonio Pichardo

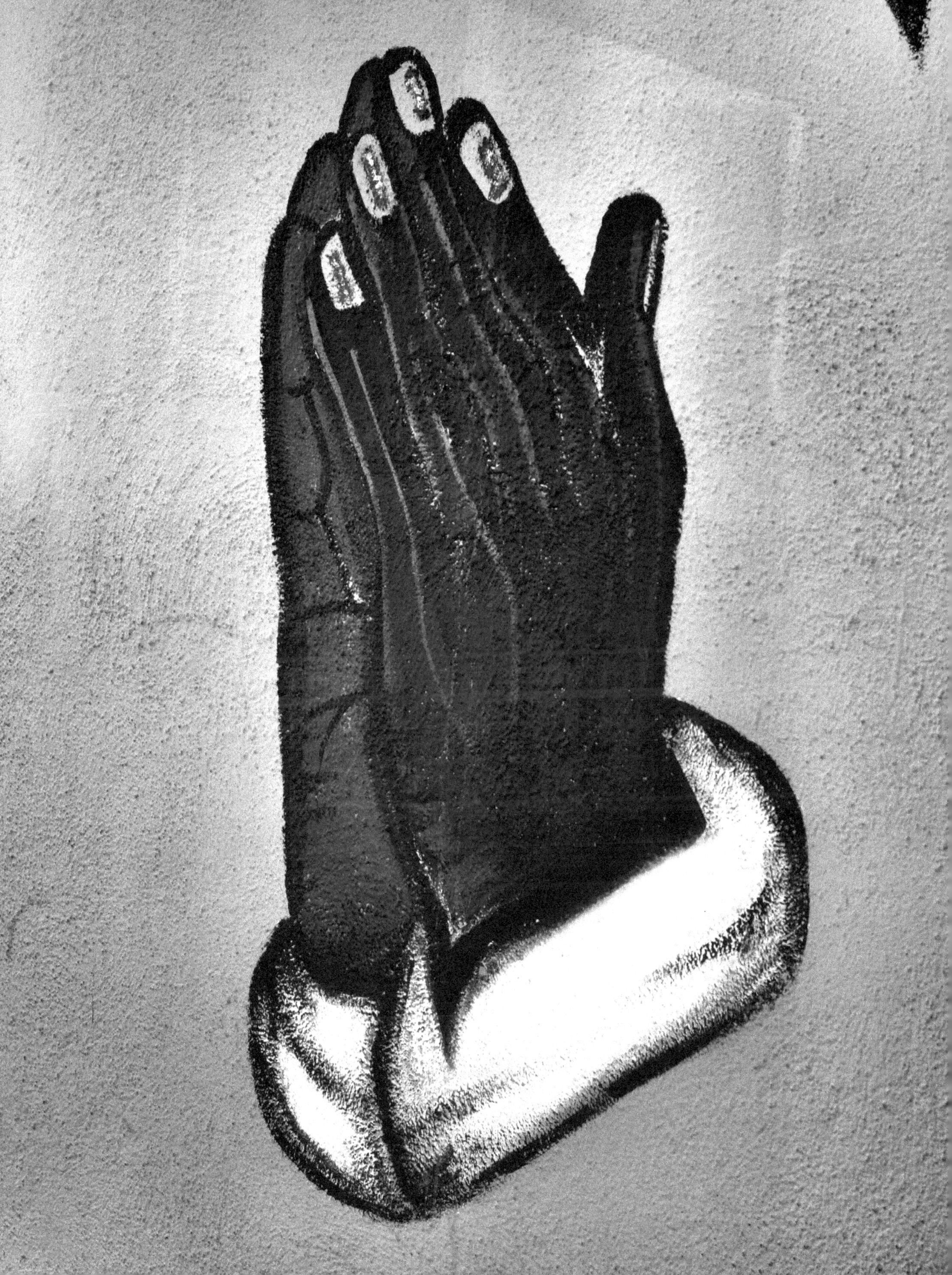

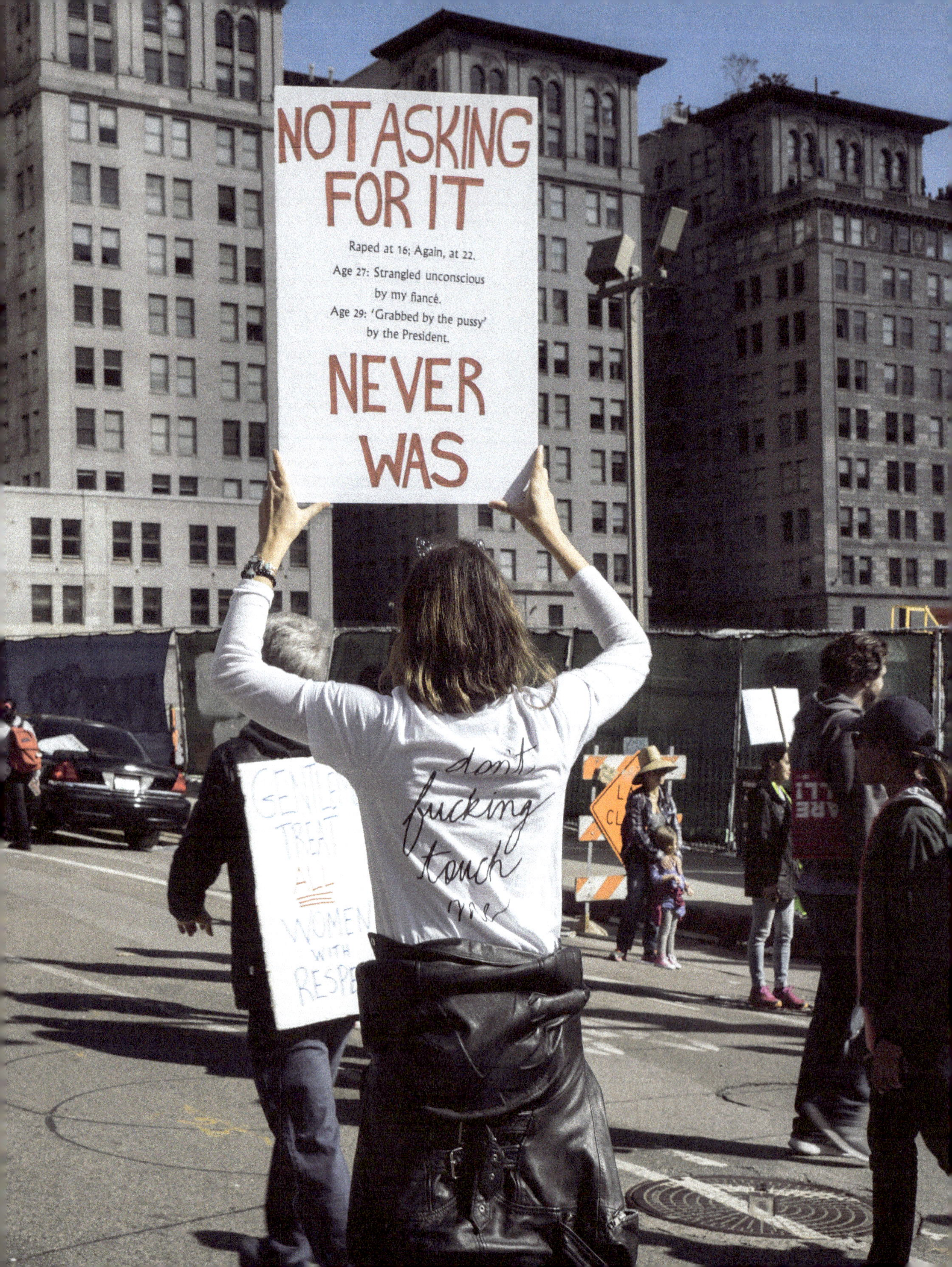
NOT ASKING FOR IT
Raped at 16; Again, at 22.
Age 27: Strangled unconscious by my fiancé.
Age 29: 'Grabbed by the pussy' by the President.
NEVER WAS
don't fucking touch

Petals of a Flower

Michelle Smith

He loves me,
he loves me not,
he loves me?!
My heart will not be
stomped on,
baked on,
gooked on,
danced on,
pounced on,
like petals of a flower.
My body, my stem trembling,
crushed within your hands.
Petals blown from your lips of succulence
and breath endlessly,
falling in suspension timelessly,
only to be swept under the rug.
My hands (are) my leaves.
Oh remember this:
Some flowers do not possess a scent or smell
perhaps you many not know and cannot tell
for my leaves and stem can crush or bend as well.

Women's March #5; *photograph*, Abraham Jaramillo

We Be Bluezin, Poem'n, Jammin, Slammin

Mello "Bluez" Houston

We Be Bluezin, Poem'n, Jammin, Slammin
in these Western streets of the Metropolitan
how you think we made-makes it?
with "terrible times" South Cali-poet Eloise says
such times influxin everything-music n churches,
rasta herb doctahs for some.
"grandma's hands" prayers for most
20 something years later?

sense rodney king pain insensed so many
n the victims added up n the authorities suited up
parents in color tell their kids to live careful
n the TV shows select free people living brashly...
contradictions mixed with social media spins
Get you some homemade Clarity

WE BE BLUEZIN, POEM'N, JAMMIN, SLAMMIN
in these Western streets of the Metropolitan
Wisdom grows inna GHETTO which is
everywhere such pain is

BE YE SEEKING
LOVE, HOPE, PEACE N TRANQUILITY
HOLY STREET-WISE CITIZENS,
Ye Must Cultivate Balance
not empty vainities
redemption song childrens

BE CREATIVE BRIGHT LIKE CLEAR WATER IS
LIKE BLESSED RAIN WATER IS...

WE BE BLUEZIN, POEM'N, JAMMIN, SLAMIN
IN WESTERN TOWNS O' NU BLUES REALITY

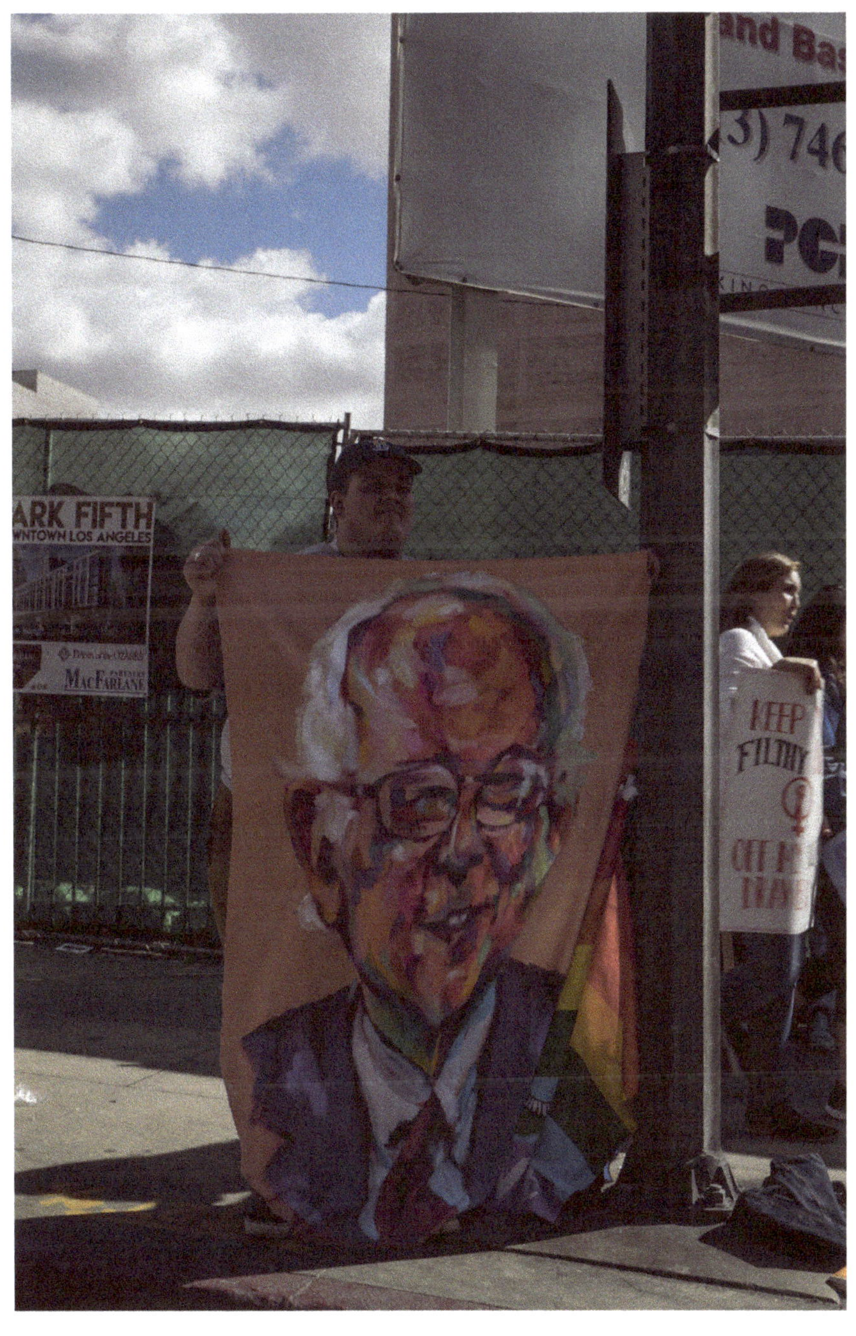

Women's March #8; *photograph*, Abraham Jaramillo

One Brick

Maggie Kane

One brick.
One big brick.
One big, grey, sturdy
Cement brick.
In raised up hands,
Heavy, over his head.
Moving up, over and down.
Down, down, down.
Towards the ground.
No, not the ground.
No, not down to the ground.
Down, to a head.
Down to a man's head.
Laying on the ground.
Laying rigid and prone.
A man laying alone, vulnerable.
On the ground.
One brick, one man's head.
They met, alas, on the ground.

Magic

David Fallon

Ordinarily I do not believe in things like magic—I'm a practical cat that has no time for things I cannot see with my own eyes, smell with my own nose, hear with my own ears, feel with my own paws. I also do not appreciate the stereotypes involving witches and brooms. But one day, something happened to make me question just about everything I believe in this world.

Humans have curious customs that make them at once fascinating, yet repulsive. They eat in the strangest manner by sitting on seats at a large board and using metal sticks to shovel their food into their mouths bit by bit as they wipe their mouths with small sheets of paper. And the food they eat! Not just meat, like us, but all manner of roasted and boiled plants, seeds, and leaves. Then, when they are done stuffing themselves they sit on another seat in a room full of water where they do their nasty business before using smaller sheets of paper to wipe their backsides. For the life of me, I will never understand human ways.

There are other customs which make better sense, such as their propensity to sleep on humongous flat pillows. These sleeping places are amazingly comfortable, sort of what you might imagine heaven to be like. And even though I have an aversion to sleeping next to them because they move a lot and make horrible breathing sounds, I sometimes cannot resist curling up close on that strange cloud of nirvana.

As cats we live in two worlds: the inside world constructed by people full of unnatural things and the outside world of nature where the trees and grass grow. My mother taught me to be respectful of both places, to be thankful for the people who serve us and to show reverence for the creatures on the outside. As tempting as it is to kill for sport every bird and mouse I see, my mother always told me: "You must only kill to live."

People are very different from us about killing. They kill for many reasons, some of which I will never understand. They kill because things get in their way. They kill because they disagree with each other. They kill because they enjoy the fleeting feeling of power it brings. Worse of all, they kill because they want to take what is not theirs. They are destructive—breaking things, knocking things down, burning things to ashes. You might wonder how

I know all these things, and I will tell you the truth. I have seen them with my own eyes.

By far my favorite human in the house is the smallest one. She calls me sweet names and sneaks bits of chicken and fish under the table for me. When she was younger, she would bundle me up and put me in a small carriage. I didn't mind, because it was a safe place to take a nap while she took me around the neighborhood. When she became a little older, I would sit next to her on the couch while she wrote numbers and letters on pieces of paper—something called homework. She fed me every morning and evening, and stroked my fur with the softest, gentlest hands. If I thought it were possible to love a human, I would definitely say that I loved her.

The day I learned magic was real was also the day I learned the depth of my feelings for her. The destruction of our neighborhood and home happened suddenly and quickly. In the dark of night, I watched from the living room window as a large group of people came down the street with violence in their eyes. They smashed windows and took things from the stores and homes in our neighborhood. More and more people came, like a colony of ants slowly surrounding a lump of melted ice cream. At the time, no one else was home so I hid underneath the girl's bed.

After hours of shaking in fright at the loud noises, my people finally came home. I could hear the girl running from room to room calling my name. When she came to her own room, I peeked my head from under the bed and meowed at her. She quickly bent down to scoop me into her arms and marched into the living room where her parents were. It was late at night, and all the lights were off. The large window in the living room glowed from a bright, orange fire that covered the building across the street.

The girl's father was yelling orders, and her mother was shuffling items into a bag, things like pictures, papers, and drawings done by the girl. The girl was gathering up some of her favorite toys and putting them in her backpack. She added my food bowl to her stash. The father yelled something that was familiar to me: "Go! Go! Go!" The family scrambled to leave the building.

There was smoke in the stairwell and it was very hot. Just like the one across the street, our building was on fire. Fear got the best of me, and I struggled to get away. "No!" shouted the girl as she gripped me tighter. Suddenly we were outside in the open air, and I could not help myself. Without thinking, I squirmed from her arms and bolted into the darkness. The girl's scream tore through my heart.

Somehow I ended up at the top of a very tall tree where I could see everything around me: the people, the fires, and even my family. They were trying to make their way down the street. The girl's dad had dropped whatever it was he was carrying so that he could hold both the girl's and the girl's mother's hands. The girl was crying loudly, and I could hear her from the top of the tree. As I began to regret my hasty actions, I tried to figure out how I could get back to my family. That was when the unthinkable happened.

A small group of men broke away from the larger crowd. They grabbed the girl and her mother and yanked them away from her father. Her father protested, but one of the men pushed him down to the ground. The girl's scream was sharp and piercing. The man hovered over the father, a glint of steel rising with his hand. Clearly this man was prepared to kill. And that was when the magic happened.

All at once my body took over for my mind, and before I knew it, I was soaring through the air toward my helpless family. As I was wondering what I would do when I finally hit the ground, my body suddenly became lighter than air. My front legs flattened and expanded. My back legs elongated into long, pointy claws. Or at least this is what I told myself in my mind. In my mind, I saw myself picking up my family in my huge talons and flapping my mighty wings to knock down the men before lifting them into the sky.

A few days later, I woke up safe with my family in a place they called hotel. They gave me some tuna and water, and I went back to sleep. I was so very tired. To this day, I am not exactly sure what happened, but I know that my family is safe.

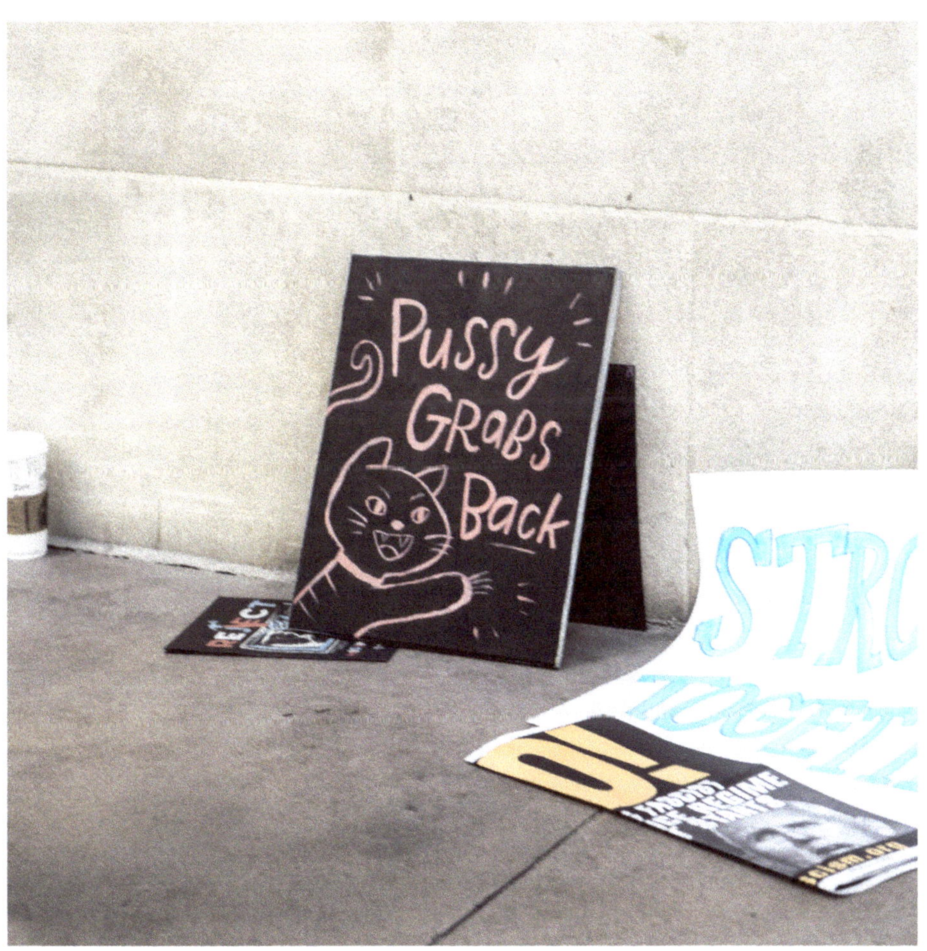

Women's March #13; *photograph*, Abraham Jaramillo

Nana's Heart

Michelle Smith

Shiny sterling silver
Sparkly and cool to the touch
Inside soft red velvet
A jewelry box reminds me of Nana's Heart
No music, no jewelry, nor an empty find.
Memories open of childhood past and love,
For our matriarch,
Beautiful teacher, disciplinarian, and kind.
Stored up like heaven's treasure.
As a little girl, our days spent together were
Collect in a jar,
As if fireflies,
And our nights glowed like moonbeams.
Imaginary sand flows freely from my hands.
My yesterday is gone in a flash.
All grown up and too old to pretend.
My memories sustain and remind me of way back when.
When the world grows cold,
These crown jewels of moments have me captured forever in time.

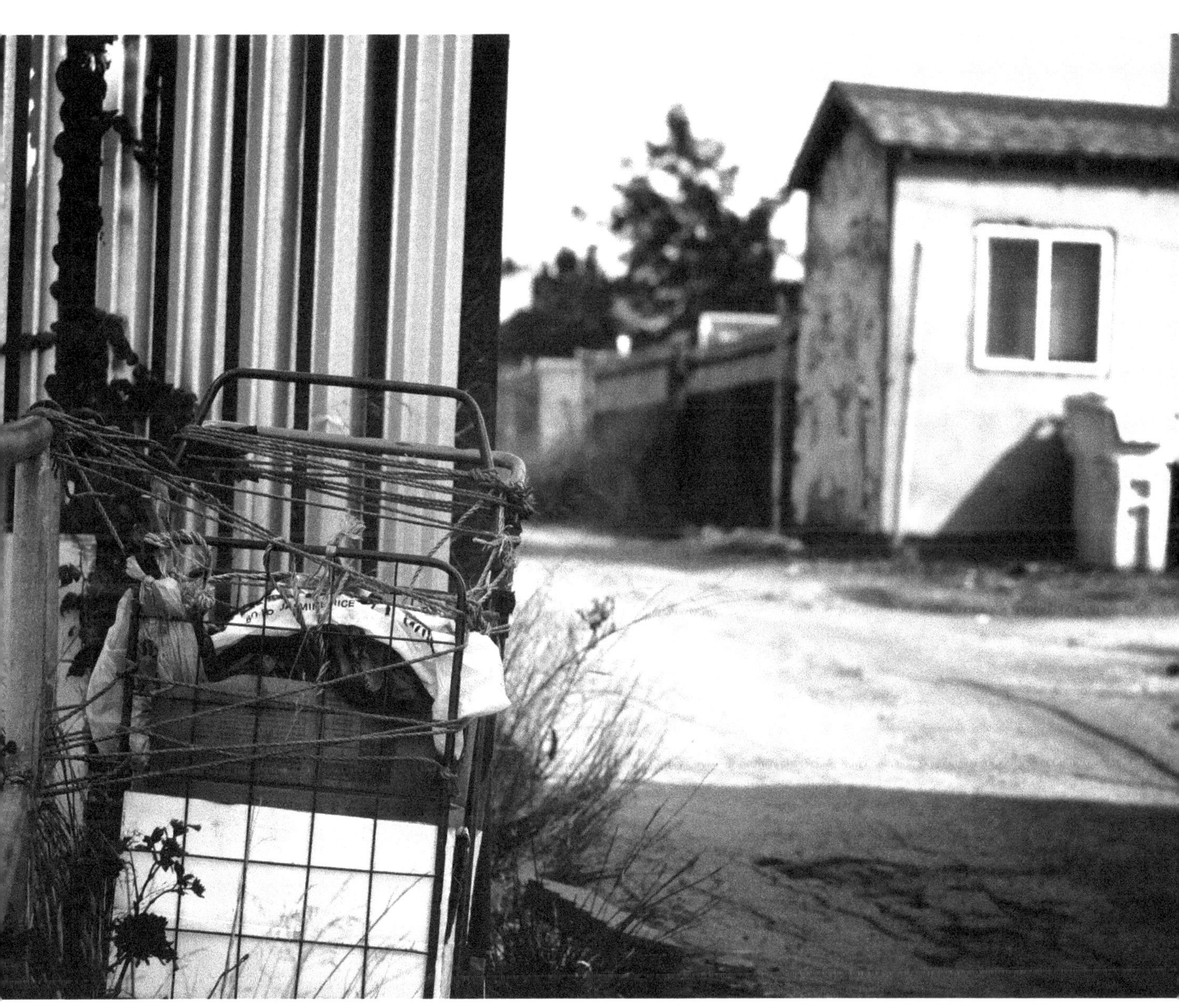

Stash; *photograph*, Luis Antonio Pichardo

Avocado Tree

Jennifer C. Fuentes

There was an avocado tree that belonged to our neighbors behind our duplex that became so large it spilled over into our back yard. For many years, my mom didn't have to buy avocados. She would go out with a little basket and pick up the avocados that landed on the dirt or in the back of my dad's old pick-up truck. She would never pick from the actual tree. She considered that stealing.

And everyone else that lived in our quadruplex did the same, even our neighbors who collected stolen hub caps and car stereos. They never picked from the tree. They picked from the ground like everyone else, even when the avocado hung at arms length. No one touched it until it reached the ground.

No one knew the neighbor whom the tree belonged to. No one ever talked about him or her either. No one ever said how lucky he was to have such a beautiful avocado tree, like how my mom commented of the lemon tree at the house next to Magnolia Elementary. "Look how big they are, little suns ready to be squeezed." Or the dark red rose bush that she would so casually caress, and then pull, to then put a red rose behind my ear. She did this often in the afternoons on our way home from school, which inspired me to pretend to be a flamenco dancer. "When we have a house, I'll have flowers in every color," she'd say.

We ate avocados, and that was that. And when we wanted one and there were none on the ground, we simply didn't have any, even when we could so easily pick one, and no one would ever know. I came to the conclusion that everyone knew something about the avocado tree, or the owner, that maybe I didn't know. Maybe the tree was cursed, but that couldn't be because we still ate them and we were fine. Maybe it was because avocados are not as beautiful as flowers or as aesthetically pleasing as lemons? Or maybe it was because we already had them and we didn't appreciate them, even if it was from the dirty ground where my dad did his oil changes and where dogs sometimes pissed. The fact that no one was tall enough to reach them also made no sense since my dad had an old ladder leaning against a wall in the back yard that anyone could use. No one ever answered my questions.

One day, riots broke out in my neighborhood. Our apartment complex was lonesome among a row of businesses, and that day, many people stampeded into these businesses and took all they could. From my balcony I could see a kid who ran out of the Thrifty's Drug Store doing a balancing act with about ten tubs of ice cream in his hands. I saw a group of sweaty fat boys struggling up a hill with a rat-brown-colored couch. People came out of the video store with bags full of many days worth of entertainment; and some ran the streets with bottles of stolen liquor that others tried to wrestle from them with little success. Crowds congregated and played a bloody game of tug-of-war over stuff; pink, greasy donut boxes, diaper boxes and bags of carrots now scattered and stepped on. Stores were ransacked, every last bit of what they had was squeezed out of them, and because that was not enough, they were then set on fire.

But the back of our apartment complex was quiet, almost peaceful. In a panic, my mom instructed me to take the clothes hanging from the clothesline and throw them into a bag, just in case. When I opened the back door, I saw an older woman, hair in a long, salt-and-pepper braid, standing at the top of my dad's old ladder by the avocado tree with a strainer in her hand. She wore a raggedy, pleated, knee-length magenta dress that exposed the green varicose veins on her short, thick, brown legs. She was picking from the tree! The strainer was full of avocados. She was graceful, steady on the ladder and humming. She spoke to the surrounding sparrows and a hummingbird, who in turn, communicated with her. Everything happening at the front of my home was now blurry, mute and slowly forgotten. I watched her and couldn't, nor did I want to, say anything. After all, it wasn't my tree. She came down the ladder and saw me standing by the clothesline. She grabbed an avocado from her strainer. "Would you like one?" I nodded my head.

She was toothless and beautiful. "Okay, have a good day, mijita."

I went back into my apartment where my frantic family was trying to get themselves together. At my window I followed the lady with her strainer full of avocados. She walked through the smoke and flying glass bottles, the looters and rioters. She walked slowly but with perfect posture. She walked this way, occasionally dropping an avocado and picking it up. I followed her through the crowd until she disappeared.

Agüero

Luis Antonio Pichardo

Pájaro pescuezo torcido
yo te miro
tirado en mi camino
como presagio,
agüero de justicia
en Los Ángeles donde
ya no vuelas, ya no
cantas cucurrucu
ni acurrucas los
sueños de libertad
que queman el aire
ésta noche, cada
noche entre incienso
de pino, pirul y piel
de bronce y chocolate.

Préstame tus alas,
no para huir sino
para convertir
tu plumaje en
pincel y escribir
tú nombre sagrado
igual como pinto el
mío y ella
en protesta
contra el mundo
y los dedos
corporativos
que suelen juntarnos

en cadenas de frivolidad
y dulces químicos
agujerantes de color
rojo 44.

Pajarillo amigo,
yo te he visto
y aunque las hormigas
se tragaron tus ojitos
me has dejado
el esqueleto de tu
acción: te pinto
paisaje de revolución.

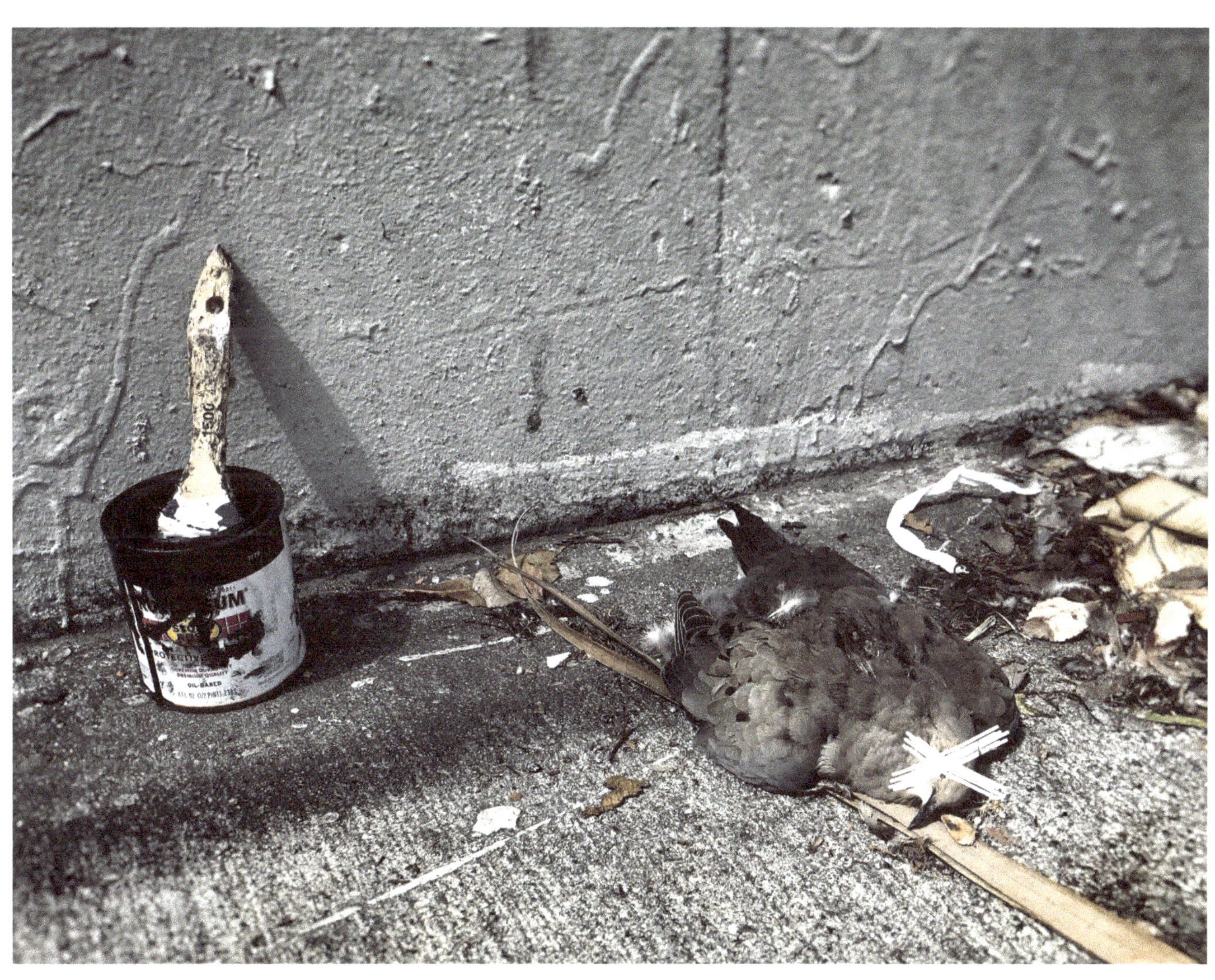

Agüero; *digital illustration*, Luis Antonio Pichardo

To Be An Artist Like Me: Faith Standing...

Mello "Bluez" Houston

when i was a little mello i was dancing with my brothers on 31st Street inna back yard & on the sidewalk out front. We ate spegetti o's and anything Miss ann cooked. she was like really "old" to us Texas to L.A. transplants. she was a "hoodoo woman" her sister, our great aunt, Aunt nita said, from Central Avenue days of colored glamour.

our mother was naturally & super pretty like nancy wilson, but she cried a lot. we had some magnificent moments on the block of beginnings. johnny still dance like those days... me too...

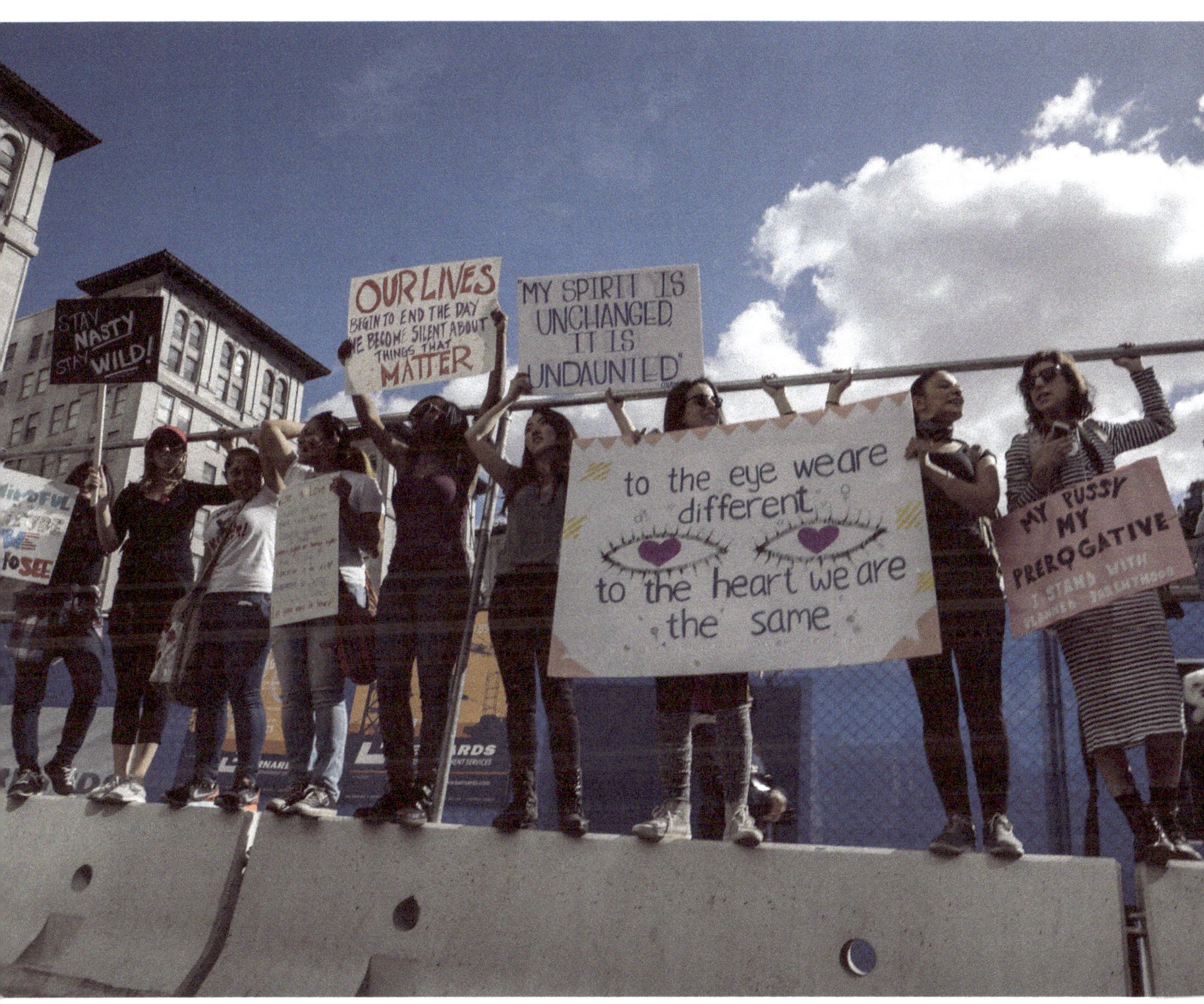

Women's March #11; *photograph*, Abraham Jaramillo

Homage

Tina Fallon

Honoring of an individual
A person of great importance
usually.

Living or dead
My person is alive
and well.

She is a spirit
My spiritualist
My leader through
Lives educated choices

My mentor,
who taught me about her
School Daze,

I appreciate you.

Sappho Don't Have To Twerk, But...

Mello "Bluez" Houston

Sappho Don't Have To Twerk, But...
She Might Have 2 Work If She Wanna Make It Inna Hood
Where Some Hurtin folks Is Up 2 No Good
If She Go To Let-mirth wearing a reggae mama skirt
She may have to Skank amidst sidewalk herbalist rituals dank
Sappho's a Poetess we spoke of in writing class
On 39th Street n Western. Where swagg n smoke are king
Actually by MLK King Street which was Santa Barbara St b4
Where Jimi Hendrix & Sam Cooke @ a nearby bar
The California did-funkay music Roar
Little Richard came thru the door
& declared himself most pretty
"Good Golly Miss Molly"
B4 yall was born
L.A. still gots "Mo Bounce"
Without our nu negrito meztizo soul glow
There's be no fresh world music stews made
Don'tcha know
Yo Sappho, Can you even dance wit yo flow?

Trumpenstein

Susan Chavez

I will never question
my ability to resolve.
Like the first drink after the heat of a sunburned patch,
I am relived

(This will be dealt with!)

I will not gasp in anguish,
instead I will thrust a death blow
to the neck of the next villain
who steals my family's water

(Do you hear me!)

I will acknowledge the strife
but I will emancipate the fear
and realize a passionate resolve

(Can You Feel It!)

I am mother
I will fight you.
I will remove you from my children's path.
Your poison will not run through our veins

(We reject you!)

Women's March #3; *photograph*, Abraham Jaramillo

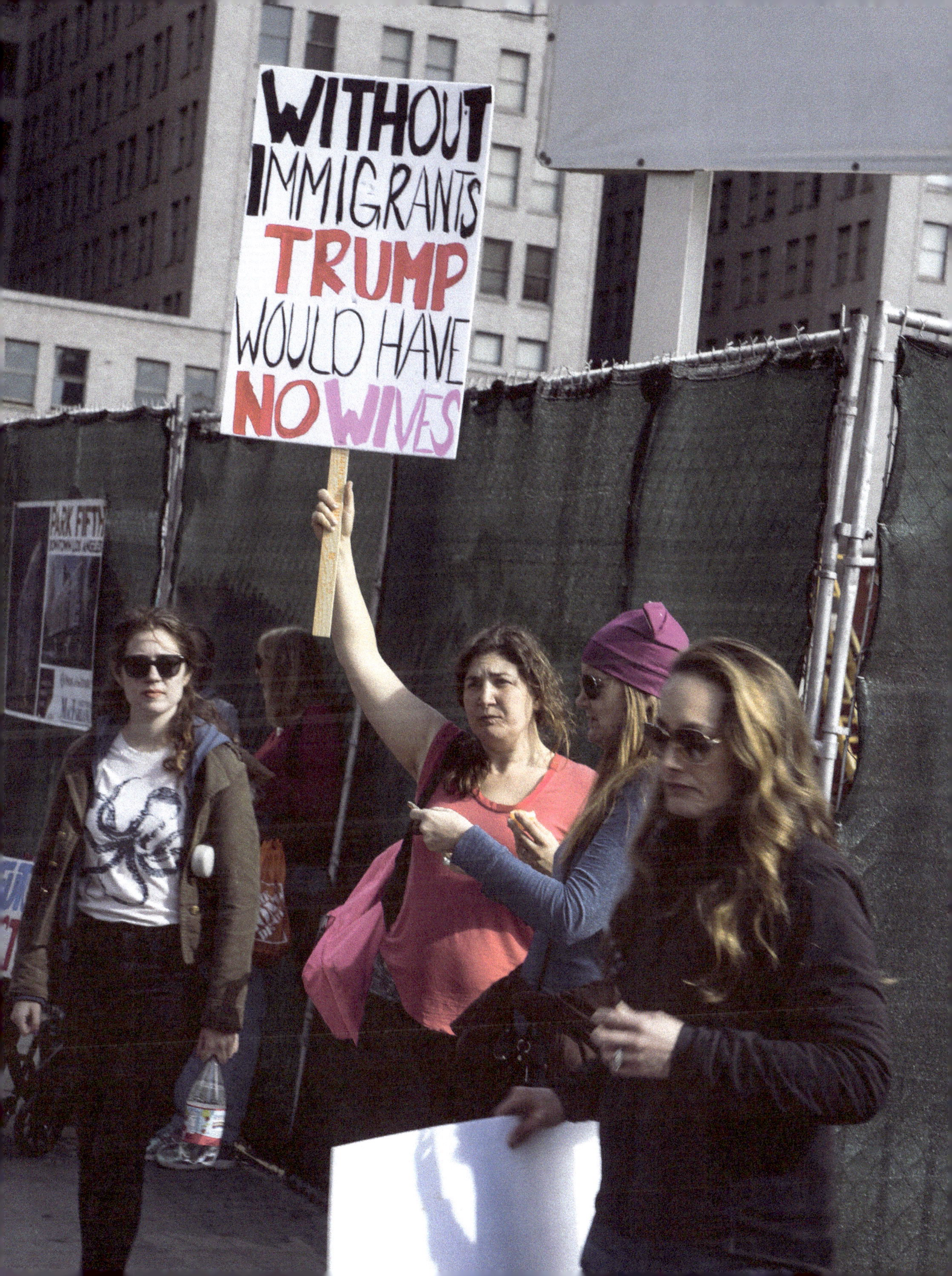
WITHOUT
IMMIGRANTS
TRUMP
WOULD HAVE
NO WIVES

N.A.F.T.A.

Luis Antonio Pichardo

Smoke outside,
smoke inside,
chronic
misgivings of a man
with no job.
They say a computer
can do my job
better than I can
so I'ma do
the best job I can
collecting cans
after emptying them
on my tongue.

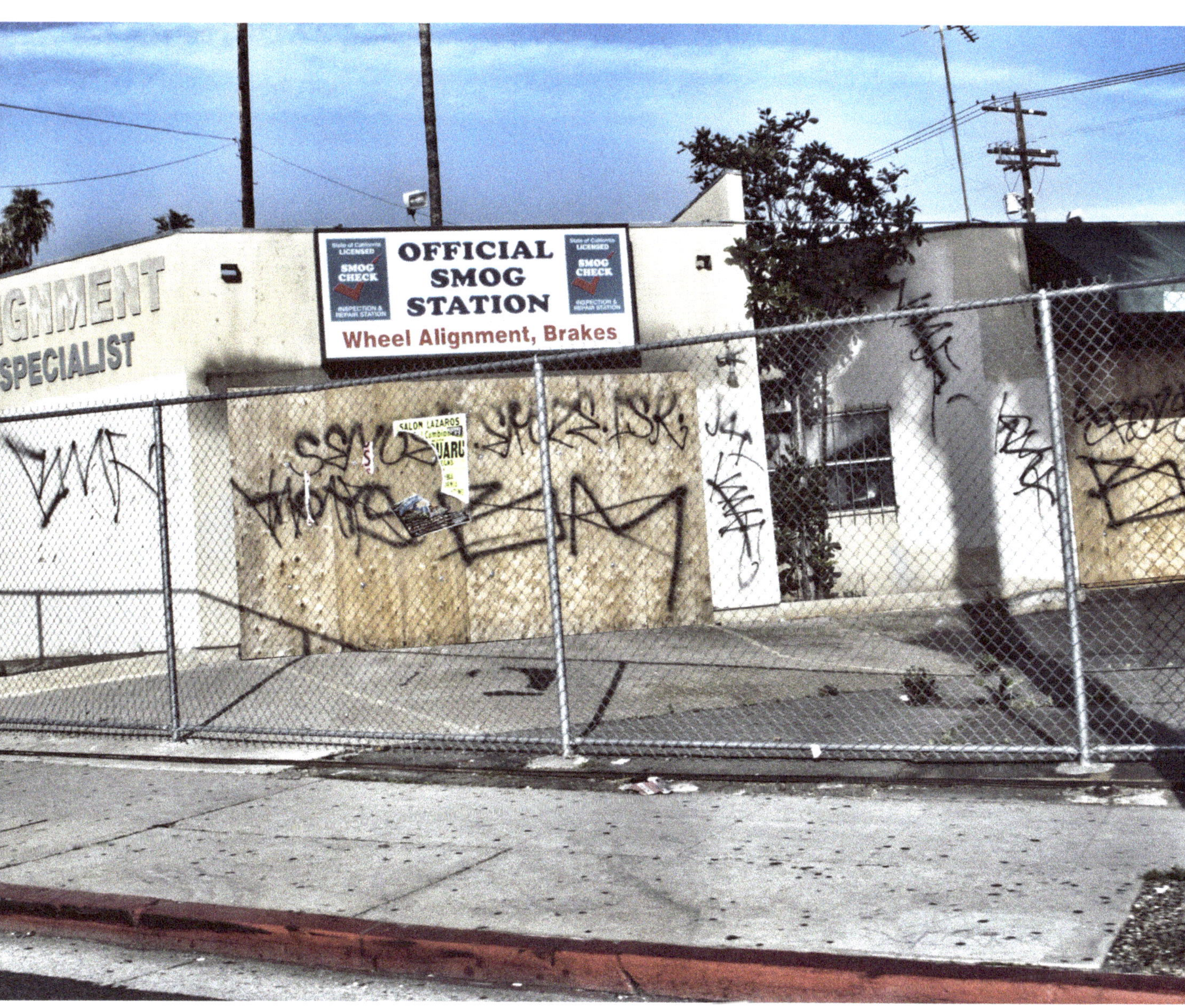

Closed (for business); *photograph*, Luis Antonio Pichardo

Consider The Pen

David Fallon

full of the black blood
of writers past present and future
yearning to be put on the page
like the words of Angelou:
there is no greater glory than
bearing an untold story

consider the pen

an implement deceptively small
filling empty sheets with hope
beyond wars of guns and bombs
spilling words that change hearts
words that create meaning
words that give warning
like the words of Bradbury:
you don't have to burn books
to destroy culture
just get people to stop reading

consider the pen

which when put in the right hand
can transform
can change the collective consciousness
can expose and dispose of hypocrisy
freedom by stroke of ballpoint
justice at the tip of a pen
to paraphrase the words of Dr. King:
the ultimate measure of a writer

is not where he stands in moments of comfort
but where he stands at times of challenge and controversy

consider the pen

its opposite power
to oppress through ominous signature
to taint innocent pages
with hate and violence
to strike at the defenseless and powerless
with ridiculous rhetoric
with vain attempts to subjugate
through multi-social mass media madness
posting Trumped up statements
filled with layers of lies

consider taking that pen

wielding it like a righteous sword
pressing your voice onto paper
bold lines of courage
lines that refuse to submit
lines that refuse to back down
lines that refuse to quit

remember the pen

and everything it has done for humanity
and everything it will continue to do

Dance It. Write It. Say It. Pray It.

Mello "Bluez" Houston

Dance It. Write It. Say It. Pray It. Dream It. Make It. Imagine It. Have It. What? Self Love. God's Love. Hopeful Love. Dance It. Sing It. Write It. Speak It. What? Freedom. Truth. Dignity. Forgiveness. Courage. Humility. Sanity. Deeper Humanity. Help Somebody. Dance It. Faith It. Never Quit Being The Best You Believe... The Best Is Free. Free? Yes. Love Is Free...

OK. Me been on one 2day. Now......
Chill... dance it......

Women's March #2; *photograph*, Abraham Jaramillo

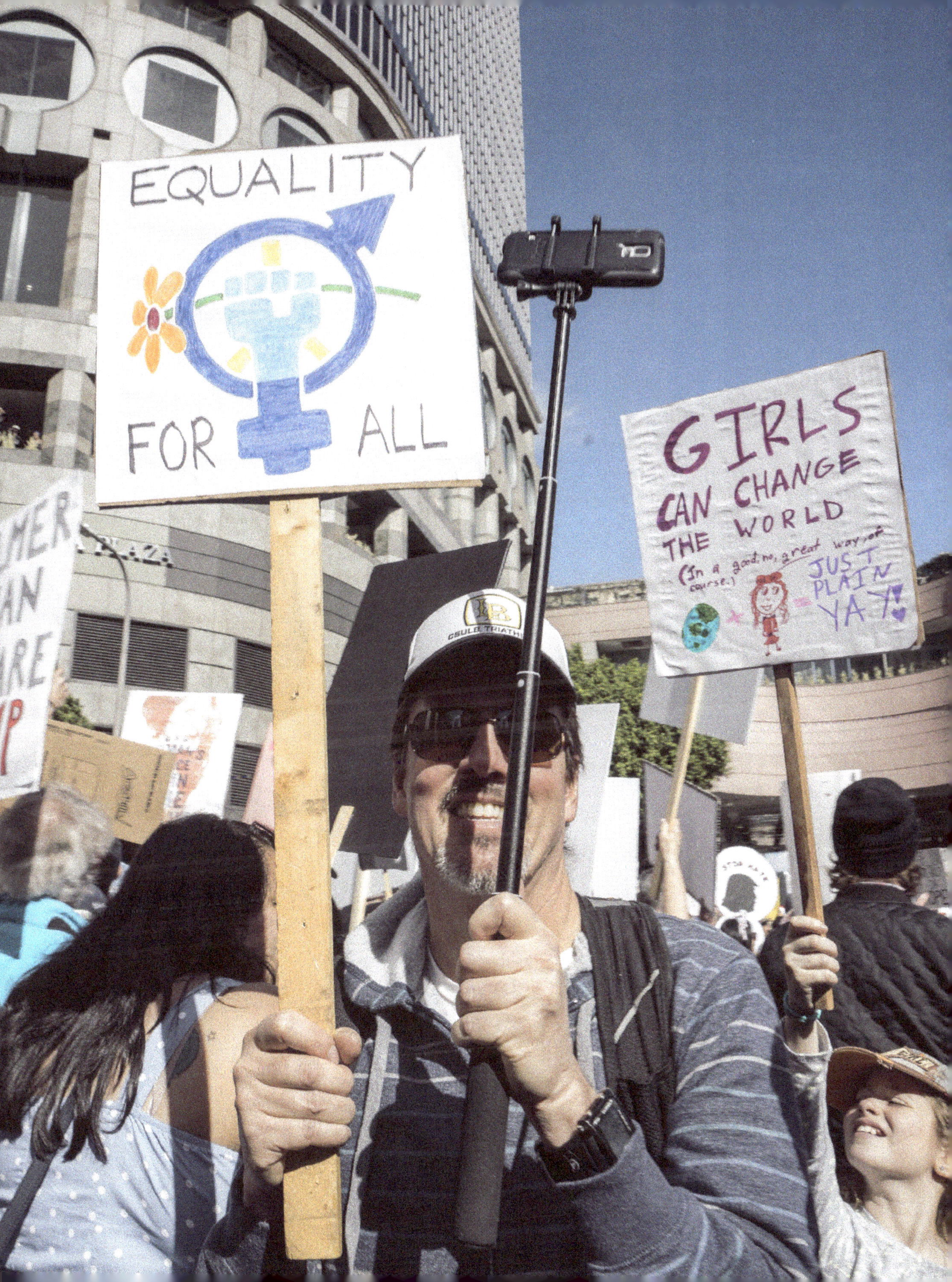
EQUALITY
FOR ALL
GIRLS
CAN CHANGE
THE WORLD
(In a good, no, great way, of course.)
JUST PLAIN YAY!
CSULB TRIATH

Dear Sappho
(Response on Elise Klein Healy)

Abraham Jaramillo

The sound of chaos
takes precedence
for a moment, but (as it must)
life will continue.
How can we expect
to be the same
(as you were) is not the same
as you are.
And so, we find ourselves
ever changing (forever).
What will come out
these terrible times?

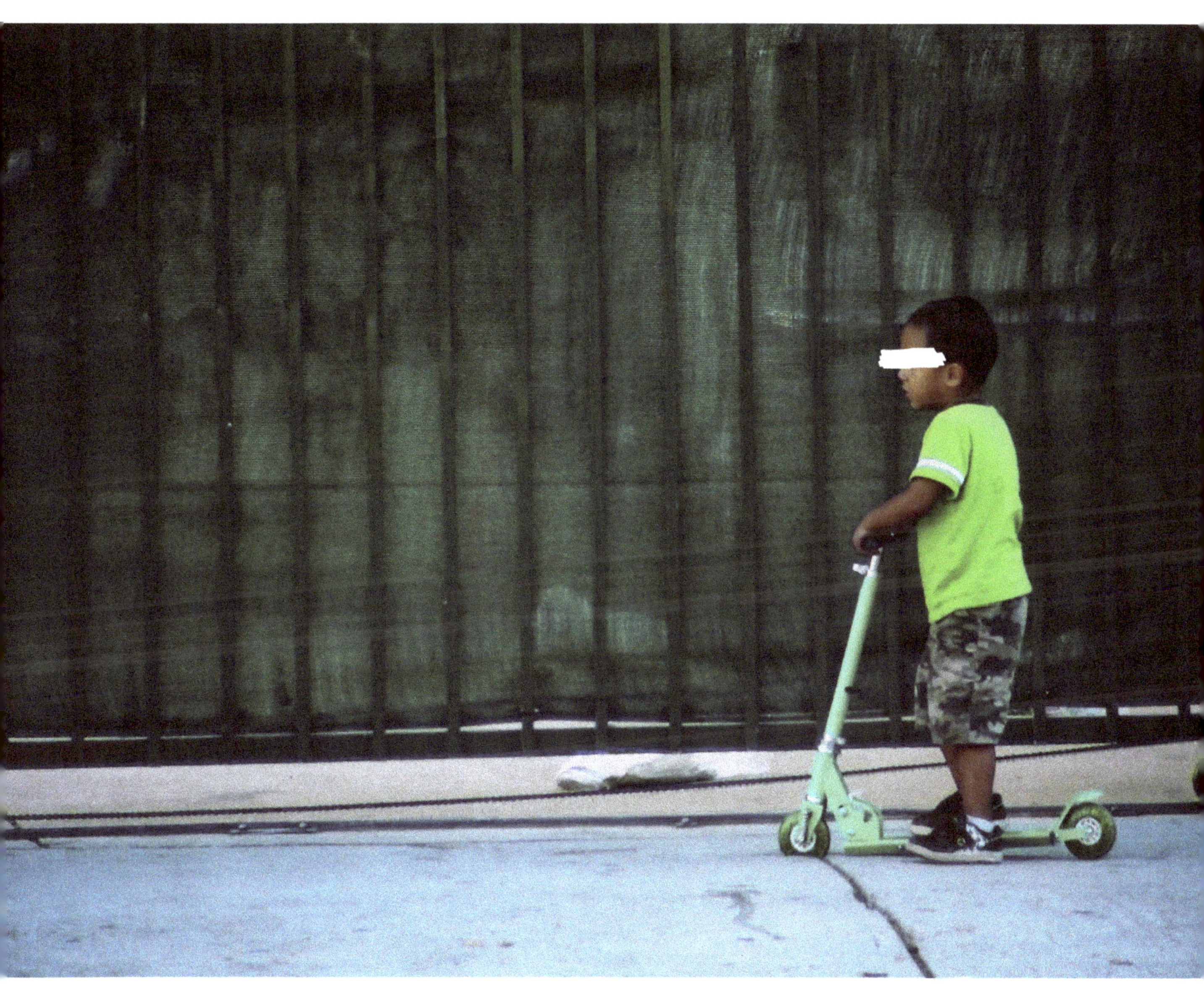

Green, Green (modified); *digital illustration*, Luis Antonio Pichardo

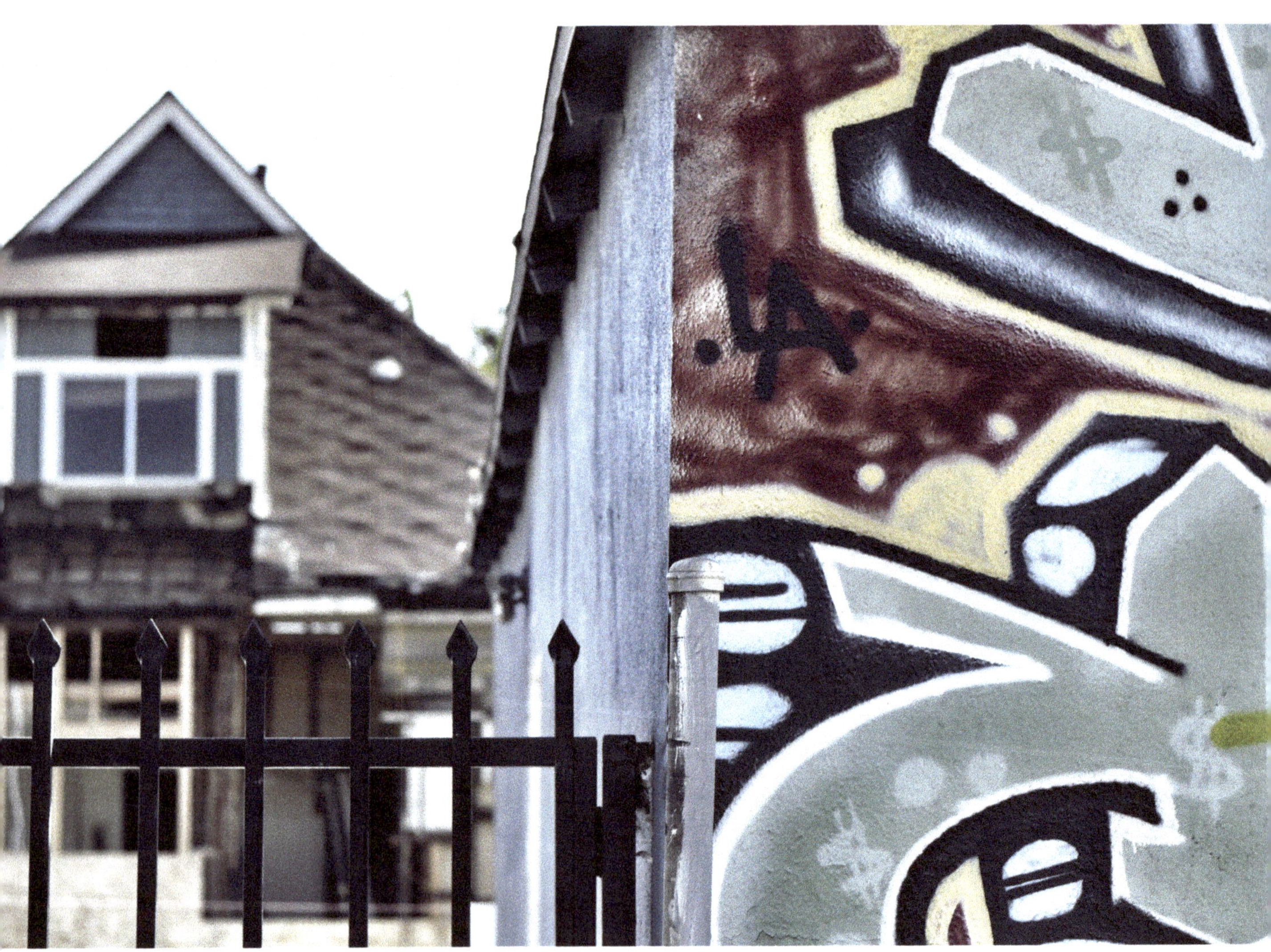

L.A.; *photograph*, Luis Antonio Pichardo

Los Angeles

Maggie Kane

Los Angeles, my home.
Been here half my life.
How did I end up here?
When did I notice the strife?

I remember L.A. and stars.
I remember L.A. and Watts.
The sun, the sea, the surf.
The night sky, filled with endless light dots.

Los Angeles, South Central L.A. Riots
1992 feelings of doom.
Today, tomorrow, more hope.
Forget the past, the gloom.

South Central L.A. Feels Like Harlem...

Mello "Bluez" Houston

...dixie peach hair grease. chicken & fries, sweet potato onna side
all this colored love won't hide. nothing holds us back. we got a savior mighty mighty,
that's solid fact... we do these thangs. we way back when brang to now, just to keep
company with great grand something ma dear used to know,
the world is growing. we helping...
let 'em have a parade in here just to say,
Ain't Soul Love mighty grand, ain't it? yeah...
We got nu HARLEM DAYZ RIGHT HERE...
church, church, church, dance hall,
business here must swing or it'll fall
keep the faith of what ya know
Stand to sing all...
yet see these,
beauty shops & barber places, kids wearing the latest creationz
be on a Paris run way inna minute, pants droppin & rap-being...
say it ain't so? we are mighty soul folks yet; Can U feel this Glow...

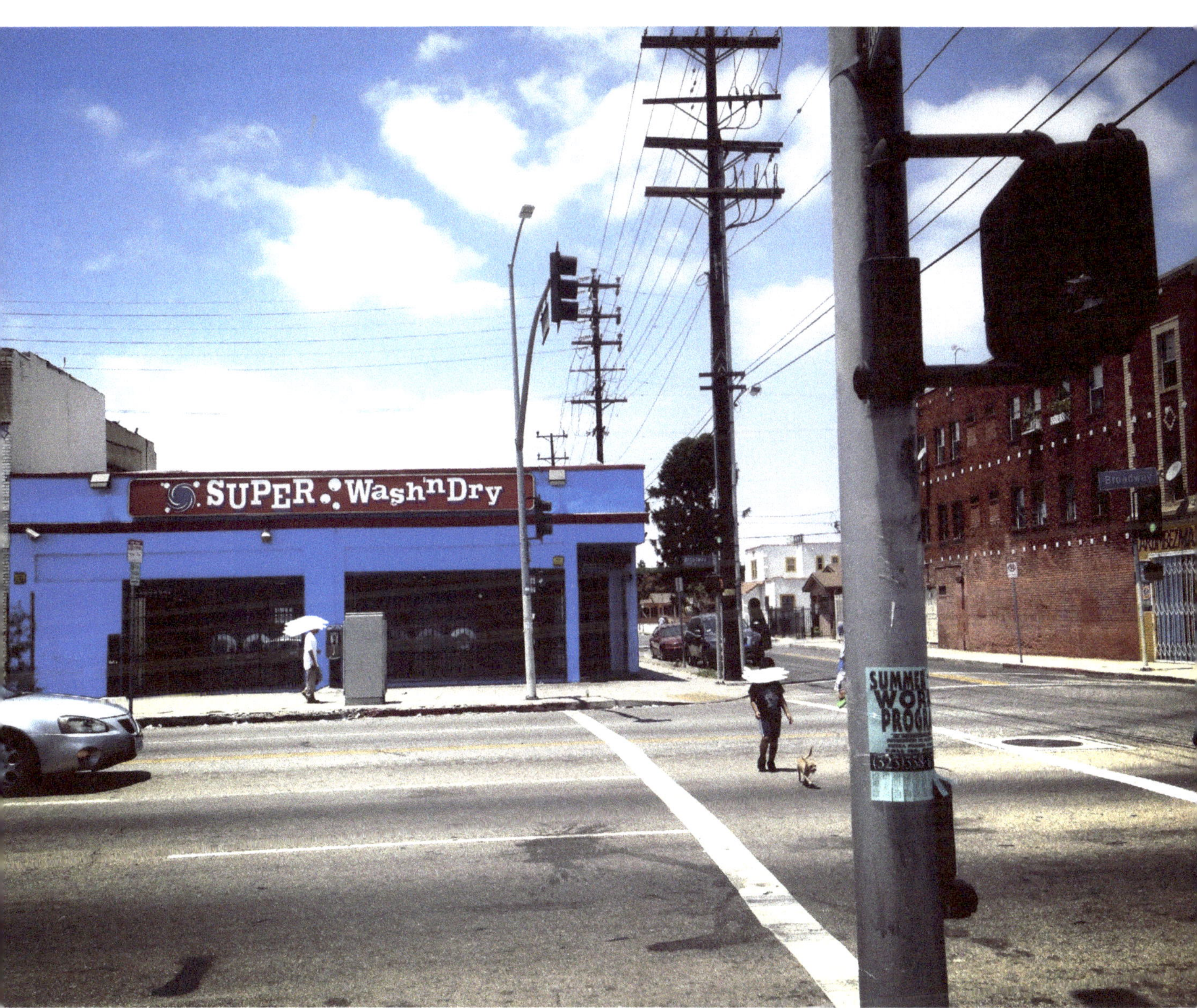

Super Wash; *digital illustration*, Luis Antonio Pichardo

Living

Luis Antonio Pichardo

Among auto body
shops and liquor
stores we hide
our belongings from
neighbors who strive
to live with dignity
as we do, but
mistrust persists,
no confidence,
dubious alliances
that don't forget
broken glass:
cars, bottles, mirrors
that showed too well
our reflection to
each other.

And police.

Watch the police.

For something
we can't trust

or believe.

Among EBT signs,
eloteros y fruteros and
medicinal herb shops
we breathe

in stereotypes and act
on welfare checks, check
cashing spots and pawn
shops for reinforced images
of financial strength:
enough to pay rent,
food by WIC,
and on occasion
a sip of Don Julio.

But the police.

Don't go out
when you should sleep.

You don't know how
deeply you'll freeze.

Within laundromats,
retail
spaces turned churches
and hose-activated
sprinklers in patchy grass,
we grasp for a wash
of our souls
and tennis shoes smeared
in blood that proverbially
runs though our streets
from the beats of
our drums skinned in hide
of our soles,
treads too worn down
by blistering
heat, cement laying
and cracked gardener hands:
a recycling center collects
our cans and glass
and pools together

our breath
for the pigs to drink.

The Puzzle

Jennifer C. Fuentes

I grew up trying to put a puzzle together. The puzzle was a 1000 piece holiday puzzle where snow covered an entire city. People welcomed the cold weather in their fancy, winter wool coats and hats; kids played in the snow and made snow men. They threw snow balls at their friends while the targets ducked for cover behind oblivious and happy carolers. There was a tall Christmas tree in the middle of it all that children and their parents decorated, and I imagined this was where parents assured their children of their overflowing college funds. Adults came out of little, overpriced boutiques with shopping bags full of Christmas presents and other goodies. The city was overflowing with happiness, privilege and a Christmas spirit I was not aware of.

I don't recall who gave me the puzzle, but it must have been a last minute Christmas present from someone who didn't care much about me. I might have seen it at the Thrifty's Drug store. I'm not sure. I looked at the picture on the box and drew mustaches on some of the women, and ladies hats on the men. I colored the snow green and purple, and when there was nothing else on the box to alter at the moment, I opened the box and scattered all the pieces on the living room center table. I started with the edges since this is what someone taught me should be done first when putting a puzzle together. I never got beyond the edges. The puzzle pieces stayed scattered on the table and my mom would put it back in the box when she was cleaning or when we had guests over. I'd take it out again, when I was bored, examine the box to see what I could still alter, work on the edges, and quit.

The scattered puzzle pieces became part of our living room decoration.

"Something looks different," my dad would say after my mom cleaned.

"I can't get her to give up on that puzzle. I find puzzle pieces everywhere and it's clogged the vacuum," my mom would say.

The puzzle took over the living room for two years. My dad attempted to help put it together during our movie nights, but he was always too distracted to focus. My mom gave it a shot a few times while on the phone but would almost always get lost in conversation or run off to the forgotten and burned rice. The puzzle was never resolved, and the picture on the box was soon so unrecognizable that even if I had had the discipline and focus to complete it, it would have been almost impossible.

Eventually, the puzzle disappeared. I saw my mom storing it in a drawer that was so hard to open and close that she used a mini-crow bar to open it. She threw the puzzle box in there and pushed the drawer closed with her foot, full force. My attempt at putting the thing together was now forever gone. I was too intimidated by the crow bar to use it. The pieces that I would find around I put in a zip lock bag that I carried in my backpack. Maybe, one day, I would be able to open the drawer and give it one more shot.

Some years later, a few days after Los Angeles had endured a massive riot, my mom and I drove for the first time to her little restaurant, which she had to shut down for a few days because of the riots. We drove in silence, afraid that what she had worked so hard for, a business that was just barely covering the bills, would be gone. The streets were mostly empty; many businesses now a hopeless pile of ashes, shattered glass riddled the streets, and some, lost in thought, sat on curbs thinking of a plan B. It was early May, but the sky was charcoal, and the agitation and outrage of a few days ago was now a deeply rooted despair that could not be healed soon, if ever.

A few blocks from the restaurant, my mom began to cry, the anxiety kicking in. She drove slower. Years of work and struggle could potentially not have mattered at all. My heart was coming out of my mouth. As we approached, we saw mounds of black residue and her little restaurant sandwiched in between this black residue. It stood strong and grounded.

That same day, back home, as I unpacked everything we had packed during the riots to potentially leave the city, I remembered the puzzle. I was unafraid now to use the mini-crow bar, and pried open the drawer. I took the box out, opened it, looked at the altered cover and scattered the pieces on the same living room table. I finally took out from my backpack the old zip lock bag with a few puzzle pieces that I had been carrying for years. I found some super glue and started putting the puzzle together the way I liked, and I started painting over the puzzle itself. I painted Los Angeles; I painted it the way I remembered it that very day.

(next page) **Roads**; *digital illustration*, Luis Antonio Pichardo

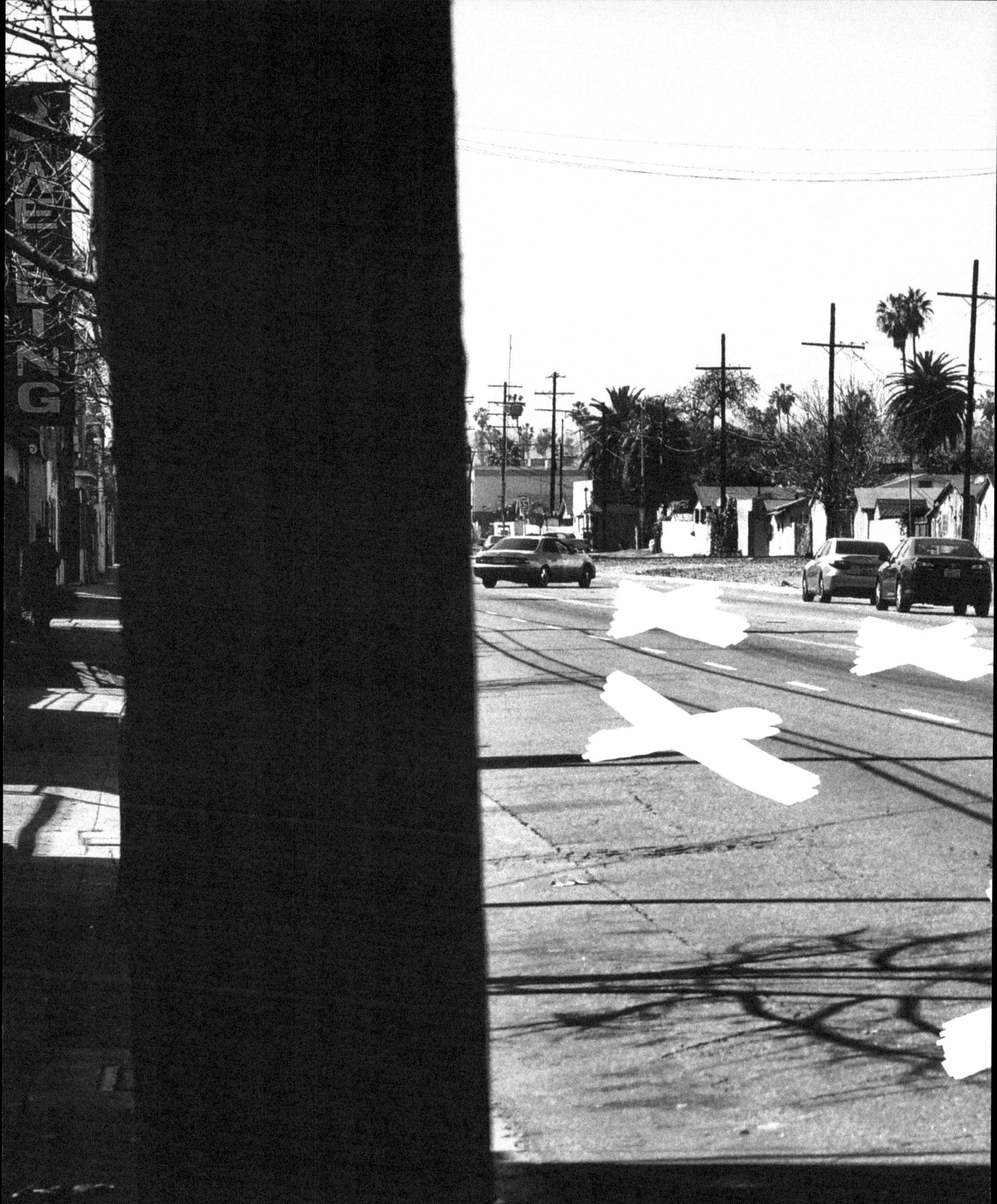

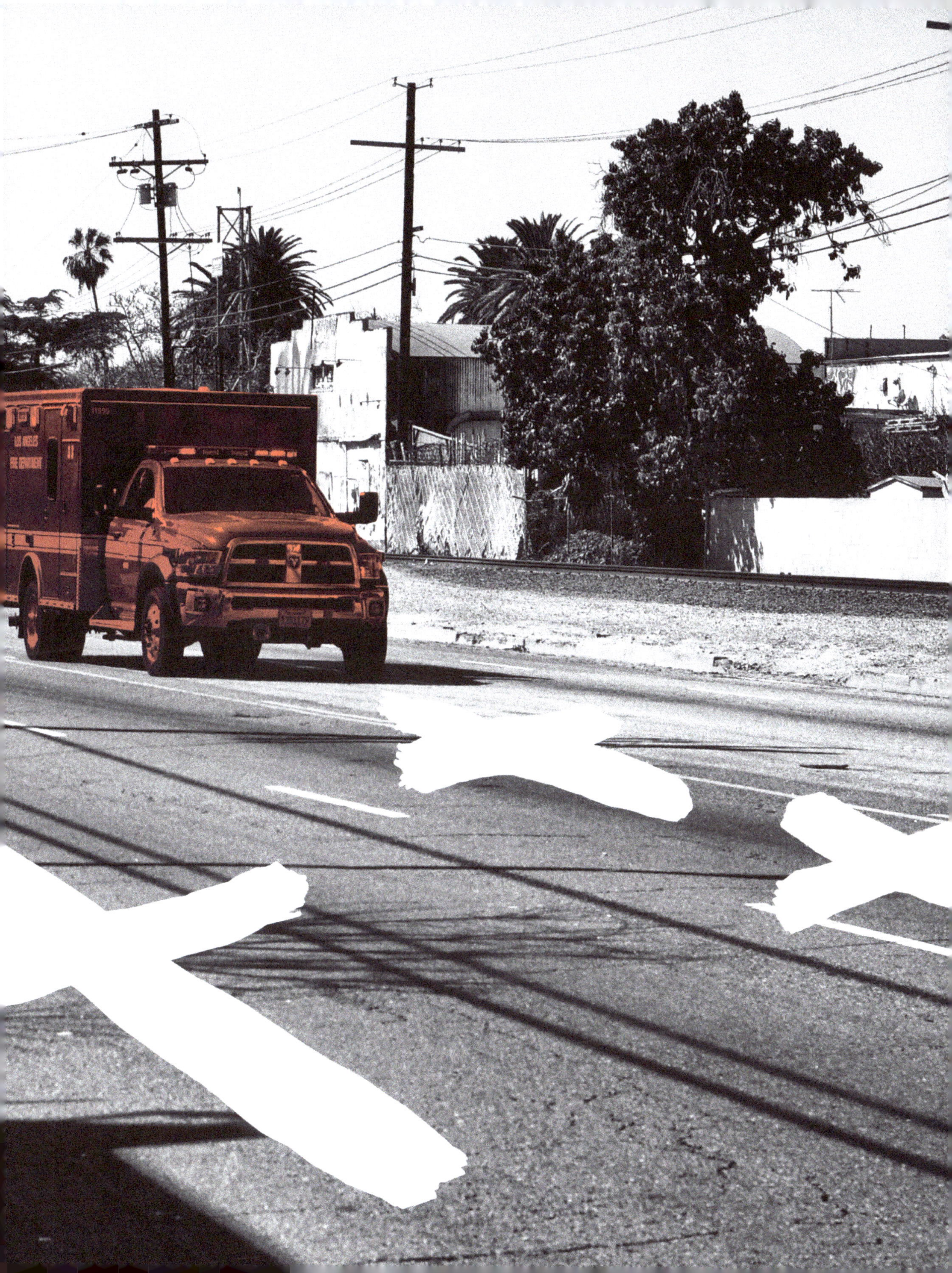

About the DSTL Arts Artist Residency Workshop program

DSTL Arts, in partnership with other Los Angeles-based organizations, partners to provide one-time and ongoing workshops in various media.

Our Artist Residency Workshops typically involve DSTL Arts staff and other Teaching Artists working together to examine issues relevant to the community, with the community; and sometimes, they're simply for the fun of sharing the power of the arts.

The Artist Residency Workshop series responsible for this publication offered creative writing workshops called Remembering the Riots with the support of the Los Angeles Public Library, Exposition Park Regional Branch. This series examined the effects the 1992 Los Angeles Riots had on our local community, and ultimately attempted to answer the question: How much has really changed in L.A.?

For more information, locations, and dates for upcoming Artist Residency Workshops, contact us by email at *info@DSTLArts.org* today.

Sobre el programa de Artistas en Residencia de DSTL Arts

DSTL Arts, en conjunto con otras organizaciones basadas en Los Ángeles, ofrece talleres en serie, e individuales, en varios medios de arte.

Nuestros talleres de Artistas en Residencia típicamente tienen como líderes el personal de DSTL Arts y Maestros de Arte, trabajando juntos para examinar temas importantes para la comunidad junto con la comunidad, y aveces son simplemente para la diversión de compartir los artes con la comunidad.

La serie de talleres de Artistas en Residencia responsable por ésta publicación ofreció clases de escritura creativa llamados Recuerdos de Disturbios con el apoyo de la Biblioteca Pública de Los Ángeles, Sucursal Regional–Exposition Park. Ésta serie examinó los efectos que tuvieron los Disturbios de Los Ángeles de 1992 en nuestra comunidad, y en fin, trató de dar respuesta a la pregunta: ¿Cuanto de verdad cambió en Los Ángeles?

Para más información, localidades, y fechas de próximos talleres de Artistas en Residencia, contáctenos por correo electronico al *info@DSTLArts.org*.

This program is supported in part by the Los Angeles County Arts Commission, a county agency, the CA Arts Council, a state agency, the National Endowment for the Arts, a federal agency.

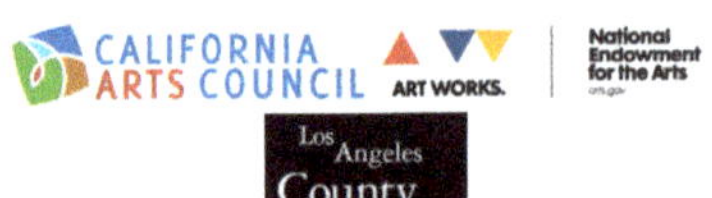

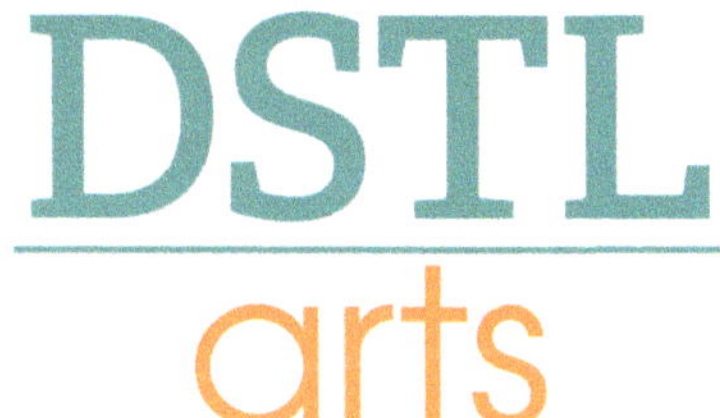

This publication was produced by DSTL Arts.

DSTL Arts is a nonprofit arts mentorship organization that inspires, teaches, and hires at-risk youth ages 16–21 years old.

To learn more about DSTL Arts, visit online at:

DSTLArts.org

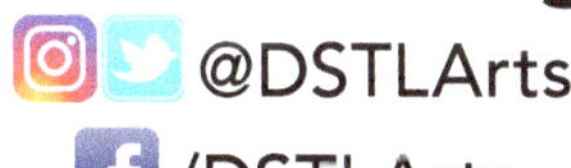

@DSTLArts

/DSTLArts

www.ingramcontent.com/pod-product-compliance
Lightning Source LLC
LaVergne TN
LVHW060631110826
845147LV00014B/892

9781946081049